ET   30416

C0-AVH-909

THE AMERICAN PRESIDENCY

The Dilemmas of Shared Power and Divided Government

Prepared for the
National Academy
of Public Administration

THE AMERICAN PRESIDENCY

*The Dilemmas of Shared Power
and Divided Government*

Ernest S. Griffith
*Former Director of Legislative Reference Service
Library of Congress*

New York • NEW YORK UNIVERSITY PRESS • 1976

030416

Copyright ©1976 by New York University
Library of Congress Catalog Card Number: 76–4599
ISBN: 0–8147–1006–9

Library of Congress Cataloging in Publication Data

Griffith, Ernest Stacey, 1896–
    The American Presidency.

    Bibliography: p.
    1. Presidents—United States. I. Title.
JK516.G73   353.03′13   76–4599
ISBN 0–8147–2961–4
ISBN 0–8147–2962–2 pbk.

Manufactured in the United States of America

Preface

The Institutional Presidency is America's central answer to the problems of "big government," problems which face all industrialized nations. This is even true if we consider only the White House and Executive Office staff by themselves. When the definition is broadened to include the patterns of the presidency's relationships with Congress, the press, the bureaucracy, the states and localities, the pluralistic public, the world—the overriding importance of these relationships is frankly terrifying. Yet the American government is supple. Eventually it seems to provide correctives—to errors of commission and omission, in the fields of procedures, substance, Constitutionality, malfeasance, even lack of skilled leadership. There are three branches; and corrective potentials in each for error in either of the other two. Notably is this true of the Executive and Legislative—for, while separation of powers defines Constitutionality, checks and balances produce accountability. Even the pendulum swings back if it goes too far in either direction.

Perhaps never before—or at least not since the Constitutional Convention of 1787—has such a brilliant galaxy of writers, scholars, and practitioners concentrated on the present state and future course of the government of the United States. For the most part—but not wholly—their attention has once again centered on the Presidency—its

trends, dangers, potential. The convening of a conference* on the Institutional Presidency at Airlie House in
the spring of 1974 brought the matter into focus. Excellent papers were prepared for study in advance. This conference was preceded (and followed) by thoughtful
studies and interpretive journalism of a high order.

The statesmanlike beginnings and the unfortunate end-
ings of the Johnson and Nixon presidencies precipitated
much of the perplexity concerning this most innovative
and spectacular of our American governmental institutions. One must go to the great tragedies of a Shakespeare
for parallels. Yet, in the contemporary scene, the play and
its denouement were played on the stage of the entire
world. The aftermath provokes on a majestic scale a
thoughtfulness and soul-searching. These have always
been the earmarks of a tragedy's elevation of action to the
level of universal predicaments and hope. They mirror
the despair and determination of humanity.

It is with humility that, as author—or reporter in search
of a synthesis—I have approached the task of this book, a
task assigned me by the Executive Director of the Academy. Perhaps my perspective from earlier years on Capitol Hill may add a bit to the thoughts of those whose chief
preoccupation or life work has been with administration
and the Executive Branch. What follows is an attempt to
bring together the thoughts of the great and the near
great—not merely those who participated at Airlie and in
the Academy's task force for the Ervin Committee, but a
not inconsiderable number of other writers.

The disagreements among these persons may be fully as
significant as their agreements, for these uncertainties
may contain the seed for public discussions in that realm
in which the politician and the expert must deal jointly
with "the art of the possible."

The Airlie conference was not the first activity of the

* Funded by the George Gund Foundation and jointly sponsored by the
National Academy of Public Administration and the Committee for Economic
Development.

National Academy in this area. Its study for the Senate Select Committee on Presidential Campaign Activities—the Ervin Committee—articulated many of the larger issues involved, and with a combination of rashness and statecraft entered into the thicket of proposing remedies.

The conference and recent writings regarding the Presidency have been understandably—but unfortunately—preoccupied and somewhat distorted in their deliberations and emphases by Vietnam and Watergate. Were these isolated instances, or the culmination of trends? Who shall say? There were mind-sets, even obsessions, against the war and Nixon, on the part of the preponderant majority of the conferees and writers on the subject. These in turn may have resulted in a disproportionate concern with safeguards against their repetition. This brought correspondingly less attention to the long-range necessity of (a) finding ways to manage big government in an interlocking society and world, and (b) finding better ways to give effect to the oversight and the constructive aspects of the adversary relationship and accountabilities inherent in separation of powers. We may, or must, assume dedication to the public interest as generally a major factor in the operations of the Presidency, the Congress, and the bureaucracy. Such dedication and such mutual accountability should lead to a constructive consensus—even in a society incorrigibly pluralistic. But the sense of mission (or missions) must be recaptured. The public interest is not self-defining otherwise.

Most of the first draft of this work was completed at the Villa Serbelloni on Lake Como. My gratitude goes to the Rockefeller Foundation for its provision at the villa (the second time in my case) of an unparalleled environment for an author. To Robert Fischelis, the Acting Director for most of my stay, and to William Olson and his wife, the permanent directorial partnership, my best thanks. To the Olsons in particular belong the congenial and helpful atmosphere which they have fostered over the years, and with which Dr. Fischelis kept the faith.

My gratitude likewise goes in full measure to Roy
Crawley and Richard Chapman of the National Academy
for the opportunity to deal with such an exciting subject.
They have been most helpful throughout the project, contributing innumerable thoughts of their own. I hope also
that the participants in Airlie will feel that their most
penetrating insights have been not unfairly synthesized.

Thanks are also due to Bryce Harlow, who had been
invited to the conference but who was not in attendance.
He has been most helpful in indicating what his reactions
would have been, and in major degree, they were taken
into account in the text.

ERNEST S. GRIFFITH

Washington, D.C.
January 1976

Contents

030416

THE AMERICAN PRESIDENCY

The Dilemmas of Shared Power and Divided Government

CHAPTER 1

The Nation a President Confronts

A President confronts a splintered and shell-shocked nation.

There were always prophets of doom. There were and are elements of great strength. But today these strengths seem to be much more in our technological achievements and our resources than in deeper matters such as national purpose or personal ideals or institutions of strength in which people have confidence.

Any analysis of the Institutional Presidency in 1976 must take full account of these strengths and weaknesses. A study such as this attempts to be would be unrealistic without a grounding in the state of the nation and the state of the world. The conferees at Airlie constantly identified elements in the here and now which are factors in a President's dilemmas and difficulties and which set metes and bounds to the art of the possible.

The author, therefore, makes no apology for commencing with a summary of these factors. Many such will be noted throughout the work when especially appropriate in the more detailed analyses of the President's relationships with his immediate staff and the other institutions which must be included as principal actors in today's governance.

To bring these factors together is to portray a gestalt

1

almost overwhelming in its magnitude. With this we begin
our study.

We have been hit by—or hit ourselves by—inflation,
pollution, lack of confidence in all institutions (if we are to
believe the pollsters), crime and drugs, energy and food
shortages (in world terms), an erosion of time-honored
ethics. Perhaps the most serious aspect of the whole matter is that even experts differ as to remedies for each of
these.

The great Constitutional safeguards of the overall
fabric of government have once again served us well. Less
well have we been served by leadership, the federal system, the gigantic bureaucracy. Time may bring a turn for
the better, but how much time is there?

Certainly the institutional organization under the Constitution has revealed serious flaws as well as shafts of light
indicating potentials. To an examination of this institutional organization, especially the Presidency, this book
has been devoted. Broadly speaking, it is a report of the
agreements and disagreements of a representative cross-
section of those who have been students of, or intimate
practitioners in, this Institutional Presidency.

But we turn first to the background.

ECONOMIC FORCES

Economic trends are baffling to a President. The whole
area is filled with hard problems and soft data—and, at
the international level where cooperation is especially important, the institutions are weak and the will toward solutions often lacking. Values of nationalism, ideology, race,
or personal ambition seem to many peoples and leaders
more important than "solutions." Personal ambition—
especially when threatened—does not hesitate to exploit
nationalism, ideology, and race. This fact is not new, and
from time to time people have suffered grievously from it.
The differences today are to a great extent differences of
scale, and hence more serious. Weapons of war, the population explosion, the oil cartel, instabilities in foreign

exchange and banking, will serve as examples. Inequalities of living standards used to be thought of as existing largely within particular nations, when they were thought of at all. Today the tensions of economic inequality are not only between nations, but also between whole groups of the "haves and the have nots." More of this later, when we examine the instruments of foreign policy.

Within the United States, inflation is in a setting which has no earlier parallel. It is taking place in a period of rising wages, heightened power of government employees in all fields and all levels, until recently a tapering demand and growing unemployment, no war, relative absence of speculation. Inflation itself is still spiraling in magnitude in many parts of the world. Large sectors of administered prices have always been with us. In the past, an abundance of food supply usually made the farmers the first victims of a recession. Today the housing and construction industries have borne the brunt, but have responded by a further spiraling of costs on the part of both labor and industry. Amid attacks from both sides, those who control our credit mechanism and our governmental expenditures are trying their best. In a sense they too are "flying blind," because so many major factors are not, and probably cannot be, under control except through the interplay of the forces of a free market. Meanwhile political demands for further government intervention are still rising. The Council of Economic Advisers has really been off base in its predictions.

In another dimension, technology itself must be reassessed. As a people, we have been obsessed with the glamour of an ever increasing gross national product. Only now are substantial elements of our population and leadership appreciating the fact that much of this gain has been because costs have not included the costs of pollution of the supposedly "free goods" of air and water; nor have they taken into account exhaustible soil and the power of the oil cartel to curtail its production and raise prices astronomically; nor has recognition been given to the obscene legacies of strip mining as hitherto practiced, or the human costs of "black lung" and disasters of deep mining. Timber harvesting has reached the point of limiting the wholesome recreational potentials of future generations.

Each of the foregoing has posed hard choices to the President and the nation and the politically explosive issue of whether to continue profits and expanding GNP as hitherto understood. Each choice is inescapable—a test of our democratic capacity, at least in the immediate future, possibly to accept "lower" but probably more healthy standards of living. Politically these economic by-products are causing an enormous thrashing around in terms of symbols, realities, and governmental institutions. Which is the more important, the quantities or the qualities of life?

On the other hand, there is a highly respected body of opinion that further growth is still both highly desirable and possible—even though it must shoulder the past costs of pollution and other errors.

Then there are the issues and problems of distribution. Some of these are egalitarian. President Johnson's War on Poverty was nobly conceived. The taxation system is under all kinds of pressure as it seeks more effective means of serving as an instrument of distribution. As fast as our system shows signs of substantial reduction of the percentage of our population living at the poverty level, the line of income as to what is defined as "poverty" is lifted. Each economic group of the population seeks to use government as an instrument for obtaining a greater share of the "pie." The merchant marine and its crews; the physicians and lawyers with their monopolistic, but sacred fee schedules; the oil magnates (with sundry devices); the dairy farmers; and a hundred other groups all operate essentially in the same fashion. The Department of Health, Education, and Welfare spends more today than the Department of Defense. It probably should, but both alike are riddled with mixtures of public and special interests.

Consumerism is on the rise. John Gardner is a hero to the intellectual; Ralph Nader, to virtually all classes except those whom his exposures threaten.

A quantum leap has taken place in the magnitude of the politico-economic forces. So wide are the differences as to remedies for the ills of these forces, so soft are the data, that many persons are dazed, resentful, or escapist. Here again are factors complicating Presidential and Congressional leadership. These lie at the root of much of the contemporary turbulence and instability in our political institutions.

CULTURAL FORCES

It is a truism to say that we are living in a scientific age. Never have so much time, money, and effort been put into research and searches for its application in technology. This has been the area of our greatest hope. Perhaps it should be our area of greatest despair. Probably most of its funding governmentally is in weaponry; in peaceful areas, in health. It has—perhaps unconsciously—been among the major forces making for integrity in thought. On the other hand, our fascination with "objectivity" and techniques has almost certainly downgraded the normative in conduct and education. Our potential in material things has expanded enormously; our motivations in human relations which determine the uses of this material potential have lagged far behind. What is claimed as logical, even altruistic, in the uses of the achievements of science, is distorted by rationalizations, selective perception, vested interests. This will surface later in our discussions of bureaucracy, the Presidency, the subsystems in Congress, with their clienteles and their counterparts in the Executive Branch.

Then too, specialization in science and technology limits greatly our comprehension of interrelationships, a complicating factor of major importance in governance.

Technology has brought urbanization and eroded the family farm. Urbanization has brought the ethnic ghetto, the decay in the central city without clearly acceptable ways as yet of dealing with metropolitan areas as a whole. Both the Department of Housing and Urban Development and the Department of Transportation are preoccupied with urban problems. Much of the work of each makes more difficult and expensive the work of the other. The first extends the credit, making more possible the growth of the suburbs. The second tears up the cities, destroying homes and rendering parking well-nigh impossible at any reasonable cost. Hence, in turn, the programs and costs of mass transit. In general, the momentum of scientific and technological change has outrun the capacity of our institutions to deal with it.

A closer look at what is happening to our values and value system is warranted. They are the seed corn of motivations in the electorate, and in those chosen to operate our governmental institutions. These values are especially important in our colleges and universities, whence come the bulk of the "brightest and best" men and women in our government at all levels. The "Watergate morality" has been profoundly disturbing, especially among the best-educated of the younger men in the Nixon entourage. Yet this need not be too surprising, because in the departments of political science (formerly called "government"), economics, sociology, and psychology (which are the most important ones for administration) the predominant philosophy has come to be positivist and "scientific." The normative so necessary for good citizenship and the "public interest" has been largely downgraded or omitted. Ethics and religion often are treated as irrelevant, and even as obstacles to "objectivity."

Then there is the "counterculture", which engaged such a high percentage of the most able among our young— and by which the Nixon administration and the Democratic "establishment" alike feel threatened, especially by its revolutionary fringe. The counterculture itself seems to have no one unifying principle, unless it be anti-institutionalism. The sex-drug syndrome, one of its principal expressions, has been rationalized as protest. Actually it ends up basically as a self-destructive, hedonistic cop-out. Its hostility to inner restraints is unfortunately shared by many in other groups.

On the other hand, there are far more hopeful sectors of the counterculture. Opposition to hypocrisy, false values, pollution of the environment, outmoded institutional rigidities; and emphasis on personal relationships, craftsmanship, simplicity in use of leisure time—all these are searching and uncomfortable critiques of the status quo. The major issue of this sector, whether to work within the existing system or not, is crucial and perplexing as a factor affecting the appeal or lack of it of government service.

Finally, there is a centrifugal pluralism in society. This reflects the multiplicity of value systems, the limited experiences of the various occupational groups, racism, and the ethnic groups themselves. This pluralism makes exceptionally difficult any sense of *national* mission—that is, the kind of unifying mission evoked by the New Deal, the two world wars, our international posture after World War II (pro–Marshall Plan, anti-Communism), and, for a brief time, the War on Poverty. The potential of a mission existed in "Ask not what your country can do for you; but what you can do for your country." The trouble was that Kennedy never once proposed the latter in concrete terms. Except possibly for the early idealism of the Peace Corps, it dissolved in rhetoric.

Perhaps a national mission can be built out of calls for redeeming the times; a better use of leisure; universal service (to society) by the young; comprehending the enormous potential of our society; even a resurrection of the American dream of equality of opportunity (as distinct from demands for "instant success"). A worldwide view of human needs requires imagination; it may evoke charity—but will it evoke joint effort and genuine national sacrifice? We have responded to the Nixon-Ford-Kissinger crusade for peace and detente, but the harpies of criticism and skepticism are never far away. But what do our would-be friends mean by "detente"?

The nagging question remains. Have we the national leadership for a national mission—even in our problems at home? Charisma is suspect in public life—a smoke screen of rhetoric and exaggerated promises. Public rela-

tions are substituted for character. Perhaps if President
Ford can really translate his hopes into a program, his
very simplicity and openness may still evoke a surprising
public response. The integrity of his private life and the
spiritual forces that have meaning for him are values not
yet dead in America. On the other hand, will the relentless
social criticism so evident in many quarters be turned on
him in all its fury—whatever his motives and whatever his
program?

THE INTERNATIONAL DIMENSION

Solution of any of the massive international problems
suffers a major handicap. A problem largely confined to
our domestic scene, however serious, at least confronts a
national government as a potential single instrument for
decision-making. But what can we do for example, with
worldwide spiraling inflation? Can the free world
economy really survive, half-inflationary and half-stable?
Yet instruments of international control require virtual
unanimity among the greater industrialized (and oil-rich)
nations to be successful.

To give a really dramatic picture of the dimensions of
the problems facing our nation—and most of the others—
which require *international* instruments to work out solutions, we need merely list a few at this point:[1] (1) the multinational corporations; (2) the oil cartel; (3) foreign exchange; (4) development of the seabed and conservation
of marine resources; (5) shortages of food, leading to
widespread famine; (6) the growing gap between the rich
and poor nations; (7) great-power rivalry, including
armaments and competing, probably incompatible ideolo-
gies; (8) peace and security; (9) air law, outer space; (10)
environmental threats; (11) population pressures; (12)
human rights, including the free flow of ideas.

Fairly effective international instruments are operative
in health and postal service, but not much else.

As instrumentalities to deal with the dozen problems

listed, there are available only: diplomacy, treaties (including multilateral), detente (real or illusory), international organizations (usually subject to a great power veto), an international law with nebulous boundaries and still more nebulous sanctions. Many of the problems listed have only just entered the stage of conferences on the subject—thus far, primarily educational. Where instruments looking toward control have been created, they are usually fragile. Some apply to certain regions only. Some require unanimity for effective action. Some are subject to great-power veto. Some require voluntary subsidies from a sufficient number of nations to make viable even their limited scope. Their fragility rests ultimately upon the fact that many of the most powerful nations hold that nationalism or ideology ranks higher in their scale of values than do solutions to the problems themselves. In other words, in this sphere of international problems—more important to us than ever before in history—the problems without exception require a multinational desire to solve them, and multinational solutions. We can at times influence solutions to the problems, but we cannot unilaterally solve them. Hence the importance of the instruments of the Institutional Presidency directed toward their solution, together with the departments and agencies whose concern they are. Small wonder that recent Presidents—Nixon perhaps most of all—directed a major portion of their time and concern toward this international sector. There is little doubt that this will continue to be true for the foreseeable future. The instabilities and uncertainties in our own instruments and decision-making processes in the international arena thus assume peculiar importance.

THE INTERLOCKING NATURE OF THE PROBLEMS AND ACTIONS

The economic, cultural, and international orders are seamless webs. So, in a profound though derivative sense, are the governmental instruments and activities concerned with them. This is clearest in the existence of an international dimension in the economic and cultural forces. A dozen departments and agencies are so concerned. Moreover, lines are at times hopelessly blurred between the domestic and international dimensions of a given problem or decision.

Looking for the moment at the purely domestic scene, counts have been made from time to time of the various interagency committees surfacing in the Executive Branch. I believe that in recent years the numbers have always exceeded five hundred. This interlocking has also reached to the White House level, in the use of "czars" or coordinators, or staff men; or counselors designed to secure interagency cooperation or, in its absence, to bang heads together or supersede them in the form of a new agency dedicated to a single purpose. National security, energy, environmental quality or impact have been among the most spectacular of the functions reaching the White House for coordination. The very expressions used—"trade-off," "interface," "negotiating society," "adversary technique"—bear witness to the impossibility of any important problem or function of government whirling in its own solitary orbit. There is thus no "perfect" solution; and the continuous search for consensus is really a search either for a partial solution or for that solution which leaves behind it the fewest casualties, frustrations, and disappointments.

We live in a dispersive state. In the earlier days the divisions were chiefly geographic disunities. Today we are a people whose political approach is largely through organized groups. Mostly these are economic or occupational. An increasing number are egalitarian: women's lib, black power, Indian rights, consumers. Others represent the future as well as the present: conservation, planned parenthood. The rise of "public interest" groups is continuing and will continue. They will play a greater and greater role. Their clientele is a dispersed one, not immediately identifiable, except at election upsets.

With one accord all these groups seek political clout in Congress and in a "bureau" of which they are the clientele. Small wonder that government is a network of interrelations between its agencies—some supportive, some combative, with respect to almost any given goal. Speaking in economic terms, we have substituted a group utilitarianism for the individualistic utilitarianism of Adam Smith and Jeremy Bentham, with each group believing the furtherance of its objectives is in the common weal. "What is good for General Motors is good for the country." The elements of truth and error in both brands of utilitarianism are the same.

There is, however, one profound difference between the utilitarianism of the early nineteenth century, and the group utilitarianism of the present day. Whereas the former theoretically was at least in the beginning opposed to government intervention, the latter has embraced such intervention wholeheartedly, when it is in its favor. Government has tended to respond by creating a network of bureaus with conflicting purposes—the dispersive state. This in itself creates the inevitability of attempting to find unifying or integrating mechanisms, to "make a mesh out of things." Call this planning, if you wish.

Cumulatively, the effect of these interrelationships has been accelerating—and lots of things have gone wrong of late. Goals have not been clearly defined. Secondary and derivative effects of a measure have been overlooked. Priorities have often been accidental. Lost motion has been very great. Planning has at best been feeble, save in allegedly single-purpose areas. When such single-purpose plans have been carried out, they have often been counterproductive in other areas. These are the roots of the governmental malaise, and its attendant lack of confidence. Society's structure has demanded uncoordinated action. Governmental structure and lack of internal coordination have in turn inevitably brought the paradox of the simultaneous lack of faith in government and the demand for more action by government.

There is a gigantic momentum, largely out of control, in technology, corporate organization, the arms race, bureaucracy. Between 1960 and 1970 government expenditures in the United States (at all levels) have more than doubled. This increase has been from 30.4 percent to 34.2 percent of the total gross national product. It is still increasing.

Can the Institutional Presidency come to the rescue?

Of late, the human factor has loomed large. The best laid plans and procedures often founder on the rocks of human frailty. Similarly the greatest administrators are usually those who enlist the full potential of their staffs. We have come a long way from the days of a rigid "chain of command," at least in civilian activities.

DEVELOPMENT OF THE WHITE HOUSE STAFF AND EXECUTIVE OFFICE[2]

The White House staff and the Executive Office have had an interesting and exciting history. The initial purpose and common thread has been to give the President a better handle on the Executive Branch. Today it is clear that there were at least two other strands of development: to react to the increasing scale or magnitude of government itself, and to find more effective ways of dealing with interdepartmental relations and problems.

Commissions of inquiry date back at least to Theodore Roosevelt. While the Bureau of the Budget under the Budget and Accounting Act of 1921 was located in the Treasury, the fact that, at the time, the Director of the Bureau was not subject to confirmation by the Senate emphasized that in reality it was to be an *Executive* budget, for which the President was ultimately responsible. Following the recommendations of the Brownlow Committee set up by Franklin Roosevelt,[3] it was transferred to the Executive Office of the President. There it remained. In 1970 it was renamed the Office of Management and Budget. Its functions have fluctuated; but with the possible exception at times of the National Security Council, it has always been the most important single unit in the Executive Office.[4]

The other notable development arising from Brownlow Committee recommendations was the explicit authorization of a staff of up to six persons in the White House itself to assist the President in ways to be determined by him. Brownlow intended great flexibility in this regard, but differentiation set in early. By the latter part of the Nixon administration the numbers had grown to over five hundred—higher than that of any previous administration.

Franklin Roosevelt also put the National Resources Planning Board directly under him. This was too much for Congress, and the board was abolished—not, however, before it had demonstrated the importance of identifying and planning for major problems of the future.[5]

World War II brought a number of war-related agencies reporting directly to the President. Eventually all of these were abolished or absorbed by the departments and agencies; or, like the United States Information Agency, given a permanent status not in the Executive Office proper.

The two Hoover Commissions, 1949 and 1955, (on governmental reorganization), represented a joint Presidential-Congressional effort. For convenience they were placed administratively in the Executive Office.

The year 1947 saw the addition of two potentially most important units to the Executive Office—the Council of Economic Advisers and the National Security Council. This latter was explicitly transferred to the Executive Office shortly after its statutory establishment as an interdepartmental committee. The CEA was part of the Employment Act of 1947, and was required to make a report at least annually to the President. The latter, with such changes as he saw fit to make, sent this on to Congress as his annual Economic Report.

The National Security Council was the first major statu-

tory recognition of the interdepartmental character of
a governmental function of universal importance. It
brought together the departments of State and Defense at
the pleasure of the President. Other interdepartmental
committees or councils were formed from time to time by
legislation, executive order, or reorganization plans. The
most important (at least potentially) was the Domestic
Council of President Nixon.

Meanwhile the practice of Presidentially appointed
"task forces" emerged, to recommend policies to the President in areas of his selection.

Within the White House staff itself, differentiation continued with increases in size. Eisenhower made Sherman
Adams his chief of staff. A military liaison advisor appeared under various titles. McGeorge Bundy and Walt
Rostow were national security advisers under Kennedy
and Johnson; Kissinger under Nixon.

Actual power began to be delegated to some of those on
the White House staff. This was first noticeable when
Johnson gave very considerable power in the domestic affairs field to Joseph Califano, Jr. Nixon brought this to its
full flowering in Kissinger, H.R. Haldeman, and John
Ehrlichman, even "layering" them over members of the
Cabinet, whom he often refused to see. President Ford
has made changes in the direction of greater flexibility in
his use of staff. Donald Rumsfeld was regarded as chief in
all but name.

Without exception, each President to a considerable extent made the White House staff an expression of his own
style and preferences as to members and usage, and of
late as to delegation of power. Overall, the history of the
White House staff has been a history of growth and differentiation, reflections of the growth in government and of
its increasing interdepartmental character.

The growth in the Executive Office has normally been
statutory, involving Congress as well as the President. The
setting up of the Space Council in the Executive Office
was in spite of the opposition of Eisenhower. It was illus-

trative of two factors in the growth of the Office—the need to lodge interdepartmental councils or agencies somewhere and, in the second place, the pressure for recognition and prestige on the part of advocates of certain new functions—a prestige which the supposed more immediate access to the President would give.

With this overview of its economic, cultural, and international setting, and a brief historical sketch of its development, we turn to a consideration of the present Institutional Presidency.

NOTES

1. See the larger list on pp. 76-78.

2. The account that follows owes much to the paper by Don K. Price, "The Institutional Presidency," circulated in advance to the participants of the Airlie House Conference.

3. The President's Committee on Administrative Management.

4. See Chapter 3 for a detailed account of its function.

5. See Chapter 18.

CHAPTER 2

The White House Staff

"The President needs help."

So said the Brownlow Committee in 1939. So the Airlie conferees say today. He needs surrogates, shortcuts, honest options for major decisions. He must work with Congress as his major equal in power. He must work within the Constitution and the law. He is looked to for leadership within the government, among our people, among juridical equals in the world at large. He needs time for thought, and protection to assure it.

His life is made up of a series of relationships, all of them important, almost all of them vital. He must relate to a pluralized public, and to the media of communication with them. He must relate to the Congress, his Constitutional equal in policy formation. He must accept the verdict of the courts as to the metes and bounds of his action. He must try to set the tone and influence the mechanism of intergovernmental relationships within a federal system. He must operate in an international setting, relating himself to his country's allies, its enemies, the third world—kaleidoscopic, ever changing—relationships with economic, military, cultural, personal dimensions. Within the Executive Branch, he must relate to the departments and agencies; he must also relate to his political appointees and to the career services. He must relate himself to emerging problems and possibilities.

He must build up around him a staff for many purposes. This staff is the core of the Institutional Presidency, and with it we begin. What is it today?

If we look at the Congressional Directory, we find that the White House Office is listed as one of the units in the Executive Office of the President. It is more usual to speak of the White House staff as a separate unit, and then retain the term "Executive Office" for those units which rest upon a specific legislative base but which are not assigned to any department or independent agency. In general, it will be this usage which we shall follow, but the line between them is blurred at best.

For a long time, Presidents have had personal secretaries and assistants, often borrowed from the departments and agencies. Wilson had his Colonel House; Franklin Roosevelt, his Harry Hopkins. This took place many years before the Brownlow Committee formally proposed and Congress authorized up to six assistants working directly with and for the President.[1] Continuity of a White House staff in this latter capacity began with the Roosevelt appointees. Actually these never were as many as six for several years.

Brownlow probably saw the President as the general manager of a great corporation whose business was government. As such, his task was so great that he needed eyes and ears. Except for routine matters, the Brownlow Committee and Roosevelt himself certainly thought of these assistants as without power—not even delegated power. They were his men and served in a confidential capacity.

Differentiation soon took place. Some were functional (for example, press relations). Some were on a subject-matter basis, such as foreign trade or intergovernmental relations. Admiral Sidney Souers served Truman in national security matters. After the Bay of Pigs fiasco, President Kennedy decided he wanted his own military consultant, and brought General Maxwell Taylor into the White House. By the 1960s, counselors would frequently attend Cabinet meetings.

The earliest use of assistants was on a series of specific assignments for inquiry or monitoring. President Truman kept a list on his desk of these assignments (including those to heads of departments and agencies), and from time to time would check up. President Eisenhower had a strong central staff of five, including Sherman Adams as chief. The others were Secretary to the Cabinet, Special Counsel, Staff Secretary, and the Special Assistant for National Security.

The numbers increased under Eisenhower. Between 17 and 35 were substantive, and there were about 250 in all.

During the 1960s the pace quickened. Decisions multiplied and became more urgent. Jurisdictional disputes grew to keep pace with the growing complexity of the government. Staffs, Cabinet members, and advisors all had their personal preferences;[2] and for a while tried to help each other, partly in order to secure help in turn. The staff's greatest role came to be in information gathering, policy distillation, obtaining new ideas from various sources, drafting of messages and speeches, designing legislative strategies.

Kennedy had a substantive staff of 22, Johnson had 33 to 37. This rose to 76 with Nixon. Using a more generous interpretation of what constituted "staff," the numbers were increased by Nixon from about 250 to over 500. There was also a change in concept as well. Power was vested in certain members—Califano under Johnson, and Haldeman, Ehrlichman, and Kissinger under Nixon. By giving Roy Ash, Director of the Office of Management and Budget (OMB), and George Shultz, Secretary of the Treasury, a "second hat" as White House Assistants, Nixon eventually tried to run the whole government from the White House. What this concept did to the Cabinet will be considered later. The effort came crashing down as Watergate closed in and Haldeman and Ehrlichman resigned.

In his first systematic reorganization, President Ford relied on nine assistants. Two of them, Henry Kissinger and

James Lynn, were to wear two hats. Rumsfeld, in addition to coordinating responsibility, was to be in charge of recruiting new personnel throughout the Executive Branch. Kenneth Cole was to be the chief domestic adviser (protem), until his successor as staff director of the Domestic Council was appointed. The other five were assistants for economic affairs, Congressional and other liaisons, speech writing and politics, legal advice, and press relations. Each had a deputy. Each (including the deputy) had access to the President. This basic pattern seems not to have been materially changed (except for the splitting of the Kissinger assignment) with the transfers of Rumsfeld and Cole.

Other important functions were also from time to time assigned to White House staff. For example, they (sometimes one person) would have a considerable responsibility in locating persons for various key positions. Congressional liaison from almost the beginning was assigned to one or more of the staff. Liaison with state and local governments came to be a regular responsibility. So did assistance in speech writing. The most trusted assisted at the policy and program level. The original concept of eyes and ears of the President, as he might wish, was never lost and in fact grew fairly steadily. It was almost inevitable that as this grew, especially in areas which overlapped more than one agency, a President would ask a given staff member who had reported to him on a problem to handle it in such a fashion—or just to handle it.

Sometimes a problem or an evaluation or a program would reach the magnitude of appointing a task force or council on the subject. This had the advantages over a statutory commission of not needing Congressional approval and of confidentiality with respect to the final report, if the President so wished it. President Eisenhower named an Advisory Committee on Government Organization, with Nelson Rockefeller as chairman. President Johnson made very great use of this device, especially before he became preoccupied with Vietnam. One analyst counted 45

task forces, with a substantial number designed to master
the bureaucracy.[3] Under Nixon, the Ash Council[4] was one
of the best known. On the basis of its report, the President
proposed the supersession of seven departments and a
number of agencies, with a much more logical grouping
under four major goal-oriented departments. The Heineman Task Force made a landmark evaluation of the organization and management of the Great Society programs.[5]

It should also be borne in mind that the White House
staff from Franklin Roosevelt's time has always been a
mixture of the political and the expert. Sometimes a President was fortunate enough to find a person who was
skilled in both capacities. Of late, especially in the expanded staff of Nixon, there were experts who tried to
play politics and politicians who tried to play the expert.
Neither of these would have been too serious, had it not
been that Nixon frequently assigned surrogate powers to
them as well.

Especially in the second Nixon administration, Congress became greatly concerned at the concentration of
power in persons who had not been subject to Senate
approval and who cloaked themselves in the mantle of
executive privilege in their reluctance to meet with Congressional committees. The McCormack Act of 1951
rather clearly needed amendment if powers were to be
delegated and exercised by the staff. Nixon began to be
queried, either by the Government Operations or the
Appropriations Committee, as to the organization and
duties of his staff. In general, he was responsive to such
questions. This left open for future resolution the questions whether or how far key appointments or reorganizations in the White House should be reported, for
example, in the *Federal Register*. So long as the staff was
relatively small, and did not exercise power except in routine matters, the disposition of Congress had been to give
Presidents great freedom. Questions at appropriations
hearings were somewhat apologetically asked, so that the

committee might"explain on the floor, if questioned by a member."

There were really only a few major issues involved by the time the expansion and powers of the Nixon White House staff came to be known. As identified at Airlie, these concered (1) its sheer size, (2) the surrogate function, (3) the effect on the role of the Cabinet members of (2). Akin to this was the two-hats role, whereby, for example, Kissinger, who became Secretary of State, until recently retained his White House position (and office space) as Assistant to the President for National Security Affairs. The Director of the OMB (Ash) and the Secretary of the Treasury (Shultz) also wore at least two hats in similar fashion.[6]

At this point we must in all fairness face the issue as to why these questions ever arose. Was it simply a matter of differing Presidential styles? While this was extremely important as one considers the greatly differing Presidents, the changes reflect much more the changes in the national and world setting described in Chapter 1. They also represented genuine efforts to deal with increasingly endemic governmental problems. Are the foreign policy problems of today's threatened and fragile peace less or more important than those faced by the unifying world wars? Do they justify the preoccupation of a President and the diversion of attempts at their solution from the normal channels? Has there been any President in recent years who has not complained about the recalcitrance or immobility of at least part of the bureaucracy, or about organizational lags in dealing with problems of great complexity and overlapping departmental and clientele concerns? We have praised the budget item veto at the state and municipal level. Do the same arguments apply at the national? The respective roles of Congress and the President in policy were deliberately designed in our Constitution, basically to require the participation of both in all major decisions. Do we still agree? Do impatient Presidents agree? What are their respective appropriate roles—and can they be defined, and, if so, how? Are we condemned to annual deficits for the foreseeable future? If so, does this mean "double-digit" inflation? Is a President elected in a landslide justified in regarding this as a mandate, or ratification of his incipient ideas, when he did little in the campaign to sharpen the issues? We shall revert to these questions from time to time, but at this stage perhaps we may give Nixon at least a B+ for effort at answering them, even though we may disagree with some of his answers and downgrade his methods of arriving at them.

Granting delegated power to a greatly enlarged White House staff was one of these methods. Are the objections to the persons chosen, the procedures used, or what?

What role do we want a President to play in policy and program; and if by chance we (in "we," the Congress is the most important single component) succeed in answering this, what instruments do we wish him to use? The White House staff and the Executive Office are clearly one of the possible instruments, whose appropriate perimeters have not yet been determined.

NOTES

1. The President's Committee on Administrative Management, *Administrative Management in the Government of the United States* (Washington, D.C.: Government Printing Office, 1937).

2. See Thomas E. Cronin, "White House Departmental Relations," Brookings Institution Reprint 213, 1971, for a fuller account of this . Originally published by Duke University in *Law and Contemporary Problems*, Summer 1970.

3. William D. Carey, "Presidential Staffing in the Sixties and Seventies," *Public Administration Review* (1969), p. 450 f.

4. President's Advisory Council on Executive Organization.

5. Presidential Task Force on Government Organization. See also Chapters 4, 16.

6. See Chapter 4 for greater details.

CHAPTER 3

The Executive Office of the President

Grouped around the President are a number of agencies, many of which have little in common save this grouping. Yet because they are parts of what is known as the Executive Office, they are quite properly often called "the inner Presidency." Like the White House staff (which incidentally can be included among them), in theory they should be there to serve him in a staff capacity in his roles of leading and governing the country.

Most presitgious for fifty years was, and probably still is, the Bureau of the Budget, known since 1970 as the Office of Management and Budget.

In the popular mind it has been thought of rather largely as the principal instrument for watching over economy in government, but at one time or another it has performed many other highly significant roles. The budget itself may be thought of still as the instrument of the President's program expressed in financial terms.[1]

In the budget cycle lie its corps of budget examiners who are assigned responsibility for particular agencies. Under Vice President Dawes, the bureau's first Director, and for a considerable period thereafter, these examiners dealt with their counterparts in the various departments and agencies. They brought to bear upon them an insistence on justification of the various items proposed.

Several profound changes have affected this early function. In the first place, more and more the departments
through their own budget officers assumed not only the
initial but the primary responsibility for filtering the requests of their constituent units. Many of the bureau's
examiners came to be pleaders for the departments to
whose financial oversight they were assigned. Then too,
the government grew vastly from the simpler days of the
1920s. The bureau came more and more to take for
granted the staffs which had been allotted to an agency
for the previous year, and to concentrate attention on the
increases and new functions. The active Presidents tended
to see this aspect of the bureau more as restrictive than
helpful.

Fortunately for the bureau, this development more or
less coincided with considerable reliance upon it by Presidents in their program planning. It was the one agency
that had the total picture and the corporate memory. But
this function was later eroded by task forces and the White
House staff. The bureau's role reached its nadir in this regard in the Nixon days. The renaming of it in 1970 as the
Office of Management and Budget was designed to
emphasize the former role, with program planning utilizing the new instrument of the Domestic Council and the
refurbished National Security Council. There was still
much reliance on the more effective and prestigious
departments.

For a considerable period the bureau had the function
of clearance of all departmental legislative proposals.
This permitted a considerable contribution to their integration. The relatively minor function of clearing statis-
tical forms and questionnaires gave still another tool in
overall understanding. These functions are still retained
in theory; but more and more often they were downgraded or even bypassed as the center of gravity in program and policy and interdepartmental relations went
elsewhere.

Over the years—and to this day—the bureau rendered
excellent service to other agencies in its management sur-

veys. President Nixon looked forward to the continuance and expansion of this role. Clearly the selection of Roy Ash as Director and as the President's assistant in reorganization matters pointed in the same direction. It could also serve the Domestic Council in managerial problem areas.

The ill-fated Planning-Programming-Budgeting Systems (PPBS) was entrusted to the bureau to cooperate in its introduction throughout the government. President Johnson had assumed its tranferability as a technique from its satisfactory results in the Department of Defense. The bureau was not ready; the instrument itself was, to put it mildly, of dubious applicability in many functions; and it will probably go down in history as an ill-fated gimmick.

Reorganizations of the government ebbed and flowed as a function of the bureau. It had an extremely able career staff in this field, but Presidents fluctuated between using this staff, and enlisting the aid of outside commissions (notably the two Hoover Commissions, the Heineman Task Force, and the Ash Council). Sometimes the bureau would lend certain of its staff to a given agency engaged in the reorganization process.

Another function was in the area of fiscal policy. Along with the Treasury and Council of Economic Advisers, it played a role in the macroeconomics of the Keynesian era. With the splintering of opinion among economists in this field, its role in government expenditure—or economy— is less certain.

In its heyday, the bureau was by all odds the most influential agency in the staff arm of the President. This influence rested in part upon the perception of its power by the departments and agencies themselves. It rested still more upon the expertise and dedication of its career staff and leadership, and the quality of the advice it gave the President. Policy and program, reorganizations and efficiency, interdepartmental disputes and coordination all were part of its function.

But the explosive nature of government, dissatisfactions

in relating ends and means, a decline in the responsiveness of the departments, the distracting and critical issues
of foreign policy which came to preoccupy the attention of
Johnson and Nixon, the emergence of alternative instruments for many of its functions, the introduction of noncareer political staff in key positions in the renamed Office
of Management and Budget by fiat of Nixon and Haldeman and Ehrlichman—all these left the Office discouraged and even stunned. Routines continued to be performed well—but even Roy Ash, its Director, moved his
desk to the White House before his resignation.

What President Ford's policy will be is still not entirely
clear as of the time of writing. Some of the earlier functions of the bureau have apparently been restored. Other
options exist. We must recognize that responsibility for
some of the transfer of power away from the bureau was
its own. Its directors were deflected from managing the
bureau to advising the President; and the bureau itself
proved unadaptable to many of the new challenges to its
traditional realm.

Of the other agencies in the Executive Office, the one
with the greatest potential is the Domestic Council. When
Kenneth Cole became staff director, he found himself
largely engaged in a holding operation, pending the will
of Congress and the new President. Its role has still not
been clarified, even under James Cannon, its new Director. Ehrlichman, to whom Nixon originally assigned
responsibility for domestic affairs, proved so clearly
unsuitable personally as well as in his alleged association
with Watergate, that the council did not have the ready
opportunity to prove itself. Egil Krogh, who was head of
an important unit under Ehrlichman, was detached and
put in charge of the "plumbers."

Certainly the Domestic Council's original objectives as
stated at the time of its formation speak to some of the
most serious needs of the contemporary government: (1)
to receive and develop information necessary to assess
domestic needs and define national goals, developing al-

030416

ternative policies for reaching these; (2) to collaborate with the Office of Management and Budget in determining priorities for allocation of available resources; (3) to collaborate with OMB and others to secure a continuing review of ongoing programs for their relative contribution to national goals, vis-a-vis use of resources; (4) to provide policy advice to the President on domestic issues. It is chaired by the President. Members include the Vice-President, the members of the Cabinet (except for State and Defense), the Chairman of the Council of Economic Advisers, the Director and Deputy Director of OMB, several of the President's counselors, the administrators of Veteran's Affairs and the Environmental Protection Agency, and two or three others. Nixon summarized its function as concerned with "what we do"; the OMB's, with "how we do it." It may well suffer somewhat from the defects of its size.

From its origin and composition the Domestic Council clearly indicated that Ehrlichman was expected to play the role here that Kissinger had played in the National Security Council. He was in the process of building a staff when he resigned. Also—given its staff or secretariat—it had potentially the necessary bite which the Cabinet had lost. It was really an enlarged domestic Cabinet with an executive director and staff. The potential was there because of its funding for staff to do what committees of the Cabinet could not do. This was to enter effectively into the area of interdepartmental coordination. The staff as a whole were quite good people, but not too well matched to the functions. It did do some early work in the areas of drug control, energy, and the economy. A knowledgeable prediction was that it would take five years for it to be effective.

Nixon pushed it publicly as a kind of Cabinet substitute which would keep all members informed and give the ones concerned an opportunity to participate in interdepartmental deliberations. Committees of those concerned could count on the council's staff to analyze their interde-

partmental problems. With this in mind the reorganization abolished several statutory interdepartmental
committees and transferred their functions to the Domestic Council.[2]

The National Security Council, which was its prototype,
belongs more properly in Chapter 7, on the President and
foreign policy. So also does its advisory body, the Central
Intelligence Agency.[3] It should be noted, however, that
the NSC can be one of the key agencies of the Executive
Office, if used as Nixon initially wished it to be but
Kennedy did not. The NSC and the Domestic Council are
potentially two of the most effective interdepartmental coordinating mechanisms in a President's possession. Their
clout comes basically from the fact that the key Cabinet
members involved are members, and that (unlike the earlier Cabinet committees) they possess a substantial staff in
their own right. They are thus in a position to develop options for their committees relatively untainted by departmental loyalties. During World War II the offices of
Emergency Management and War Mobilization were responses to this same kind of need.

The Council of Economic Advisers has the responsibility of assessing the economy, forecasting its course in
the immediate future, and recommending policy thereon
to the President. Its staff is too small to do much beyond
the macroeconomics of the situation. Its most important
responsibility is to draft the annual Economic Report
which, with such emendations as he cares to make, the
President sends on to Congress. Its chairman is a member
of the Domestic Council. Beyond these responsibilities,
the President may, and probably often does, consult it.
Potentially it might play an important role in long-range
planning—as might also the OMB, the Domestic Council,
and the NSC. Such limited planning of this character as
does take place in the inner presidency is found in these
four agencies or in occasional special task forces set up for
the purpose.

There are also a number of other agencies, councils,

and offices in the Executive Office. Still others have been there in the past, such as the Commission on Productivity and the Office of Economic Opportunity, but have been transferred or abolished or are on their way out. Several factors have accounted for their location. Some were new agencies, placed there temporarily until their ultimate disposition could be determined. Others were in fields to which a particular President wanted to give special attention at the time. Others—and this is probably the largest group—were agencies whose supporters wished for them the special prestige or access to the President which such a beachhead would allegedly assure. Often it was pressure exerted on Congress that gave them such a legislative base, with the President—or those around him—opposed. The Congressional committee of origin is assumed to have an oversight function in each instance. An example of this last category was the National Aeronautics and Space Council. Eisenhower refused to appoint an executive secretary or to call the council together. It was activated later during the Kennedy-Johnson regimes, but it was eventually abolished by President Johnson, its Congressional parent, who set up a substitute by executive order. The Office of Emergency Preparedness was divided between the Department of Housing and Urban Development and the General Services Administration. Its staff was rather lost in these agencies. The Energy Policy Office is an example of a new agency, probably only temporarily placed in the Executive Office. The Special Action Office for Drug Abuse Prevention is an example of an effort by the President to indicate this as an area of his special concern. The Council on Economic Policy and the Council on International Economic Policy are basically Cabinet-level councils with staff. They are presently chaired by the Secretary of the Treasury. The Office of Science and Technology (its functions now appearing in the National Science Foundation) did have a role in that the Bureau of the Budget had nothing comparable. It was presumed that the National Science Foundation was adequate and

available. One of its senior staff is or is intended to be a
Special Assistant to the President. The old office may well
be revived. The Office of the Special Representative for
Trade Negotiations is a separate entity closely related to
the Council on International Economic Policy. The
Council on Environmental Quality (set up along with the
Environmental Protection Agency) was basically the product of a very strong clientele group who wanted to be certain of a spokesman near the center of power. The Office
of Economic Opportunity, dating from President Johnson's War on Poverty, is in process of liquidation, with the
functions that survive absorbed by other agencies. The
Federal Property Council is a White House device, under
a Counselor, which may eventually find its way to the
GSA. The Office of Telecommunications Policy would
seem to be an anomaly. The President also has an Advisory Board on Intelligence.

Counselors, Assistants to the President, Special Assistants to the President, Special Consultants usually have
designated functional assignments and often wear two or
more hats. For example, Peter Flanigan appeared as
Executive Director of the Council on International Policy
and also as Assistant to the President. This two-hat device
can be useful in assuring that those who counsel the President have reasonably adequate staffs. On the other hand,
under Nixon, it usually meant that they were interposed
between him and the member of the Cabinet or the
agency head who under earlier Presidents might have expected that he would have been the one consulted.

Are there any distinguishing characteristics of the agencies given Executive Office status? Usually, but not always,
they have a statutory base. Occasionally, as in the case of
the Director and Assistant Director of OMB and the
Council of Economic Advisers, Senate confirmation is required. Most of the chairmen may expect requests for appearances before Congressional committees. Henry Kissinger of course needed confirmation as Secretary of
State, but not as Assistant to the President or staff director

and member of the National Security Council or as chairman of several of its committees set up prior to his joining the Cabinet. He did show a readiness to appear before committees of Congress. As distinct from the narrower White House staff, these agencies usually do have to justify their appropriations to Congress.

Because of the varied nature of the origins of these units, there is not really much integration. As one authority has put it, the Executive Office is an "artificial construct." It seems likely to remain so, subject to periodic "tidying up," if and when a President is interested.

In a paper prepared for the Airlie conference, Don Price (its chairman) raised a number of important questions concerning the White House staff and the Executive Office. Were the units and persons to be divided according to managerial tools and skills, budgeting, personnel, economic analysis? There have been occasional proposals to move the Civil Service Commission into the Executive Office—the personnel counterpart of the managerial OMB. On the other hand, would it be better to relate the units to the functional departments—national security, welfare, etc.? Or both?

After trial and error, the Nixon answer was: both. Among the White House Assistants there were monitors to check on his directives to the departments. Within the Executive Office (in the wider sense) he had located the managerial tools of OMB and CEA, but he had also put there and made heavy use of the NSC and the Domestic Council. In part this was because he thought of himself as a general at a command post, and he wanted to be in touch with his colonels. To some of his assistants he gave surrogate powers, but this raised another question which will be faced later. At this point it may be noted that these surrogates, some of whom were political, were also a layer interposed between himself and the specialists in OMB.

NOTES

1. Much of the analysis that follows rests upon Allen Schick, "The Budget Bureau That Was." Brookings Institution Reprint 213, 1971. Originally published by Duke University in *Law and Contemporary Problems,* Summer 1970.

2. See also Chapter 18 for further analysis of the Domestic Council.

3. See also Chapter 17.

CHAPTER 4

Variables and Instabilities in the Inner Presidency

The "inner Presidency" of the White House staff and the Executive Office has not jelled. Nor has there arisen any real consensus among Presidents, administrators, and scholars alike as to its appropriate form and role. The lack of consensus included also the members of the Airlie conference. It will be the function of this chapter to outline the problems and instabilities, and in preliminary fashion to summarize the varying views. However, much of the analysis in depth must be deferred until more detailed consideration can be given to the collateral roles of the Cabinet in its twin capacities as an arm of the President and individually as heads of departments. Foreign relations constitute another special problem. One's view of the responsibilities of Congress in the policy and oversight roles, and one's view of the career bureaucracy, not to mention the media, political party, and public opinion generally, are also highly relevant to the Institutional Presidency in certain important aspects. What do we want the President's role to be in our system of government? The question is insistent.

If one thinks back to our introductory survey of the complex and rapidly changing nature of our contemporary society, it is easy to understand how the profound differences of opinion have arisen, and how different the answers to the various questions are.

We are probably passing through a major Constitutional crisis—not in the broad wording of our Constitution, but in the usages and roles under it appropriate to the present day and perhaps the next ten years. The partially personal crisis of the Nixon administration and the natural tendency in many quarters to hold suspect all of the procedural and organizational changes he advocated or introduced should not blind us to the fact that he did identify the major problems to be solved. We can, within this framework, hold that he overreacted to them, that his proposed solutions were incorrect, that his motivations were seriously tainted and unworthy of his high office. We cannot dodge the questions. We can—and this is the disposition of many including this author—believe that in the areas of interrelationships of the President and Congress, and also other interrelationships and usages, the qualitites of suppleness, the pragmatic approach, adaptability to the variables of situation and key personalities, are among the strongest qualities we have developed to supplement the written Constitution. We would therefore caution against too much rigidity or too glib generalizations in our thinking. Much must be left to the style and wishes of each President, and his diagnosis of the nation and the world of his time.

With this warning, we may list the principal areas of instability in the Institutional Presidency. They certainly include accountability to Congress and the appropriate policy roles of this body vis-a-vis the Executive Branch. Within the latter, the respective roles of the heads of the departments and agencies over against the White House and Executive Offices on the one hand, and the career bureaucracy on the other, are highly fluid and very much in dispute. What are the roles of the political party, and what relationships do these roles bear to the organization and functioning of the Institutional Presidency? These are the principal areas in its external relationships in which the quantum growth in government has called in question earlier doctrine. Fortunately all Presidents, save

Andrew Jackson, have ultimately accepted Supreme Court decisions as to the limits of their power.

Because these key relationships will for the most part be left for later analysis, at this point we shall turn specifically to the inner Presidency itself, bearing in mind that none of the great questions raised concerning it can really be given more than a highly tentative answer prior to consideration of these larger relationships.

The principal questions presented by this inner Presidency may be listed as: its surrogate powers and the related problem of Senatorial confirmation of those occupying key positions, its size, what kind of agencies should be appropriately included, the respective roles of the OMB and units such as the Domestic Council. Also what are its roles in the generation of the President's program, resolving interdepartmental disputes and promoting cooperation, the monitoring of the bureaucracy, aiding selection of top personnel, long-range planning? Its internal organization is also obviously unstable, and from time to time calls for clarification.

First in order of consideration is the extent to which the President may delegate to his staff and units of his office the making of important decisions in policy and in supervision. Many would still answer this question, as did the Brownlow Committee, by saying that such delegation is out of bounds juridically, unless there has been previous authorization in law. Major decisions by the old Bureau of the Budget (BOB) carried with them the often realized assumption that the agency affected could appeal to the President. The matter would then be threshed out between the agency and the bureau, with the decision ultimately made by the President. Moreover, many press the attack further and say that such surrogate power as exercised by his immediate staff is not only illegal, but would be inadvisable in any event. No staff orders should be issued from the Executive Office except in the name of the President and in response to his expressed wishes. The undermining of the department and agency heads—especially of those in the Cabinet—would be too serious. It would be possible to meet the legal objections by working out with Congress whether additional positions should be subject to confirmation, as has been done with the senior officers in the OMB. Perhaps the staff directors of the NSC and the DC would also be appropriate for such confirmation, especially if they also served as Counselors to the President. If the office of Assistant President were ever created—and one or more of these have been suggested—these clearly should be subject to Senate confirmation. That certain of the President's staff have *de facto* been operating in such a capacity has given rise to criticism—Califano under Johnson; Haldeman, Ehrlichman, and Kissinger under Nixon. The heads of new and emergency agencies located in the Executive Office have at times required Senatorial confirmation, and it would not be unreasonable for the President to delegate their supervision to a member of his staff and to require that such use of a staff member require explicit authorization (or confirmation) by Congress.

Clearly the number of interdepartmental concerns has reached a magnitude too great, and they are often too urgent, for effective settlement by the President personally involving himself. The most important ones will obviously have to concern him by way, for example, of the Domestic Council, but many could be settled by surrogates or assistants. Franklin Roosevelt used to use the director of the BOB as his adviser or troubleshooter in something of this fashion. It is generally agreed that this deflected the director too much from his BOB statutory responsibilities. Consideration of the various solutions attempted by Presidents will be treated more at length later.[1] None has really been satisfactory. The problem is growing increasingly serious, especially as the tendency in the Nixon staff was in the direction of settling jurisdictional disputes even without consultation with the parties involved.

This raises acutely the problem of the "two hats." When John Macy, Chairman of the Civil Service Commission, served also as President Johnson's assistant on selection of key personnel, it raised few questions except from strong and able party leaders such as James Rowe.[2]

Nixon greatly extended the practice. Even Kissinger, when he became Secretary of State, for a considerable period divided his time, while in Washington, between his seventh-floor office as Secretary and his White House office as Assistant to the President for National Security Affairs. Similarly, Roy Ash had functioned as Director of the OMB and Assistant to the President for Management. George Shultz, before he left the secretaryship of the Treasury, wore about four hats! There were a number of other examples. In a sense, all of them reflected the Nixon-Haldeman-Ehrlichman doctrine of concentrating all major decisions in the White House, and the desire to tame the bureaucracy. However, there were built-in conflicts, especially as between the White House and the agency presided over.

The sheer size of the White House staff has been under severe criticism, including strictures by almost all of the Airlie conferees. There are at least two schools of thought on this. The groups of critics—and they are the most numerous—who believe that the traditional roles of Congress, the Cabinet, the political party have all been seriously impaired, believe also that cutting the size of the staff would be an appropriate way to forestall such continued impairment. As a matter of fact, a move in this direction has been made by the appropriations committees. An alternative would be by legislation emanating from the government operations committees.

These and other critics also call attention to the frictions, rivalries, vendettas, and struggles for power within the inner Presidency itself. The OMB is eager to regain some of its former functions which have been threatened by the terms of reference setting up the Domestic Council. Haldeman, Ehrlichman, and Kissinger allegedly have been arbitrary and cavalier in their dealings with persons. The first two have also been generally regarded as out of their depth as regards competence because of a relative lack of background. Kissinger may claim justification in the results attained. All reflected Nixon's distrust of the bureaucracy. Ford and Rumsfeld inherited an unstable and basically unhappy situation.

To these critics a trimming of the staff in size and power would go a long way to restore "normalcy."

The "minority report," as regards size of the White House staff, felt that this was not the real question. The real question concerns the persons chosen and the functions they are asked to perform. This reverts back to the adequacy of the Brownlow philosophy of Presidential staff roles in the contemporary world. What should and should not be done at the Presidential level? If he is to be held responsible for *both* managerial efficiency and political responsibility, then he almost certainly needs assistance which is adequate and immediately accessible. If, as the predominant, but not unanimous, opinion holds, it is the second responsibility to which his role is more properly confined, perhaps the Brownlow staff concept might still work. However, it should be evident that neither "managerial efficiency" nor "political responsibility" is self-defining. This is even more true if one tries to establish the appropriate metes and bounds of each. Some hold that the President cannot divorce himself from either.

No one questions the use of staff to monitor the bureaucracy, so as to see whether the President's directives are carried out. To do this will undoubtedly uncover examples of situations in which the Congressional understanding of the policies it enacted legislatively or its delegation of specific authority to an agency head conflicts with a President's wishes and his view of his own authority. He may also discover instances of sabotage and procrastination, based upon the bureau head's own view of what should or should not be done. This latter is what Nixon expected to find because of holdovers from the Kennedy-Johnson era. All Presidents have complained of the same phenomenon. The reaction in the career services was especially acute because they saw that Nixon, more than any of his predecessors, was transferring a considerable degree of power to overrule from the Cabinet and the

Under and Assistant Secretary level to the White House itself. This also threatened the flourishing bureaucratic-Congressional-clientele subsystems. No one questions the use of the OMB or special task forces to perform an evaluative function of specific programs, if the President has reason to believe that agency-sponsored evaluations have been self-serving. Congress itself from time to time also conducts such evaluations, and the General Accounting Office in particular is proving a powerful tool in this regard.

The somewhat miscellaneous set of agencies in the Executive Office put there for special attention (Presidential, Congressional, or clientele) obviously are and should be unstable. The suggestions has been made that they should be put under a perhaps temporary "Cabinet Member at Large," subject to Senate confirmation, until such time as their ultimate disposition is determined. By legislation or the agreement of Congress as part of a hopefully restored power of reorganization, they may be shifted at any time.

Clearly the inner Presidency has an important role to play in generation of the President's program. Members of the Cabinet and heads of agencies can and should participate, either on the President's request for their recommendations or through the National Security Council and Domestic Council. The President himself must clearly have the last word as to the program's content. He will do well also to take into account the OMB, CEA, and also his political advisers.

Public relations are clearly in part a function of his staff. What can be delegated to agency heads is fluid. They must not "make waves" in this area without clearance.

At present the organization of the White House staff and the Executive Office is very much in limbo awaiting directives of the new President.

This leads to the final element and instability—the style and wishes of the President himself. A Kennedy can dismantle the Eisenhower structure, but he can learn from the Bay of Pigs and from counsel that the principal

abiding elements of the inner Institutional Presidency
must be restored. He preferred to settle many controversial issues of policy after listening to adversaries arguing
with each other. Johnson commenced his Presidency in a
whirlwind of establishing task forces, taking counsel, and
acting. In the end he was so preoccupied with Vietnam
that he had to delegate most of the domestic scene to
Califano. Delegation of power to staff had begun with
Kennedy. Eisenhower preferred an orderly use of
Cabinet and staff, the last President (except possibly
Ford) to attempt a serious resusciation of the Cabinet as
an operative institution. He was the only one of our last six
Presidents with previous large-scale administrative experience. Nixon, especially after what he regarded as his 1972
mandate, went far beyond any previous President in concentrating supervision and policy in the White House.[3] He
really wrestled with the problem of the institutional inade-
quacy of the government as he found it, particularly as to
how to command and control its several parts in a pluralistic society. His choice of assistants—at least many of those
he kept—contained serious flaws—or worse. His comprehensive program was largely aborted as Watergate closed
in on him. Meanwhile he had weakened all the internal
constraints.

The analyses by the Presidential (Heineman) Task
Force on Government Organization and the President's
Advisory (Ash) Council on Executive Organization have
so figured in discussions of the inner Presidency and
actions taken with regard to it, that we shall close with a
brief summary of their respective findings and recommendations.

The Heineman Task Force was concerned principally
with the organization and management of the Great
Society programs. Its findings were:

1. The target problems of poverty, discrimination,
    urban blight, air and water pollution are not the
    sole concern of any one department. They will not
    yield to a series of isolated program efforts.

2. Federal social programs remain badly coordinated in Washington and in the field because of (a) wars over jurisdiction, (b) related programs, failure to mesh in target areas.
3. The social problems are in the field, but administration is centralized in Washington in autonomous units below the Presidential and departmental level.

The causes were:

1. The President lacks continuing institutional staff to deal with wasteful programs and jurisdictional conflicts; to control and pull together various programs in Washington and the field; to reflect Presidental perspective in areas requiring interdepartmental cooperation.
2. The President lacks staff to plan ahead, to evaluate, and to develop his annual legislative program in a long-term perspective.
3. The President does not have the staff to keep in touch with the governors and mayors.
4. The departments do not have full control of their programs because they do not have staff to dominate their managerial levels.
5. The field structure lacks any effective coordination.

Recommendations:

A. In the Executive Office:
  1. Office of Program Coordination for Domestic Affairs.
  2. With an adequate field force.
  3. Office of Program Development.
B. In the departments:
  1. Strengthen the office of Secretary in program planning, budgeting, and coordinated field management.
  2. Reduce the number of clientele-oriented Departments.
  3. Cabinet members to put his own men with power in the regions.
  4. Unify department operations.

    5. Consolidate manpower activities in HEW.

    6. Locate field offices in the same town.

The general diagnosis held that the President and Cabinet members were really impotent as matters then stood.

The Ash Council listed the following needs of the White House staff and Executive Office:

1. A better instrument to develop policies and programs.
2. A better instrument to develop legislation and budget.
3. Assignment of organizational responsibilities.
4. Resolution of program management responsibilities, especially in interagency differences.
5. Evaluation of progams.
6. Development of executive personnel.
7. Creation of an information system for the President.

It recommended a "Domestic Policy Council" to work through flexibly constituted "program committees." Also a reduction of the number of units in the Executive Office.

President Nixon attempted to carry out the substance of most of these recommendations. For one reason or another he did not "follow through" in many key instances.

NOTES

1. Chapter 16.
2. See also pp. 154, 174.
3. See Chapters 17 and 18.

CHAPTER 5

The Departments, Agencies, and Commissions

The Cabinet is fast becoming obsolete. Cabinet members are not.

In other words, the time-honored idea that the Cabinet as such was the appropriate group to advise the President fell of its own weight. This fall was universally recognized at Airlie, although the conferees looked hard for a meaningful role. Presidents will almost certainly continue to use the Cabinet as a forum to which they can toss certain of their high policy proposals to test the reactions or through which they can communicate directives as to budget objectives and guidelines. A President can be photographed with the Cabinet, and add to the prestige and kudos of the individual members. It can be a part of the visible government; but as a unit it will continue to play little or no role in its operations or policy guidance. Why? Its decline represents a major readjustment in the power balance and the usages under the Constitution.

In the first place, these are busy men—all of them. In the second place, many of the important decisions on which the President wants advice involve two or more departments, but not all of them, and not usually a majority. As such, the advisory function is better handled by groups of those concerned. The Domestic Council and National Security Council would seem to be the most

appropriate vehicles for this. Committees can be formed
from them on an *ad hoc* basis; their staff can do the analyses and prepare the options. When the President, the
council, or the committee makes a decision, a committee
of Under Secretaries or other persons carry it out. These
instruments can be enriched (as appropriate) by adding
agency heads, members of the White House staff or other
units in the Executive Office. Even prior to formation of
the Domestic Council, a congeries of functional "cabinets"
were taking the place of the Cabinet as a whole.

In the third place, the Secretary himself would usually
prefer to take matters of importance concerning only his
department, directly to the President. If the other Cabinet
members are present, they are either waiting their turn to
present their own problems, or disclosure of such
problems may inhibit the original Secretary by stimulating
jurisdictional jealousies. The President will always retain
the option of referring a problem to a larger group, or of
asking for more data, perhaps from the OMB.

At its best, whether serving as a sounding board for the
President's ideas and problems, or for informative
purposes, when one agency was planning to launch a
major program, briefings of the Cabinet were and could
still be in considerable depth. Eisenhower made a valiant
effort to use it in such fashions, and sometimes succeeded.
When Franklin Roosevelt tried to use it for counsel or
debate, one of his aides claimed that no Cabinet member
ever told the truth about his own agency. Treasury simply
did not want Justice to know what it was thinking. On the
other hand, if Cabinet meetings are regular and are used
for important discussions or briefings, especially by the
President himself, and if the secretariat or a White House
Assistant follows up the decisions, these meetings still
have potential as a vehicle of communication. There may
be no other chance for these people to see each other.
Also they may have an opportunity to see the President
individually before or after the meeting. If the Domestic
Council should pass out of the picture for any reason,

then only the Cabinet would be left—clumsy and ineffective though it is for communications of these types.

Yet when all is said and done, in recent years its members have become increasingly disappointed and disillusioned, for the popular image of the Cabinet had been of an agency at which matters of high importance were discussed. Almost the only real Cabinet discussions held by President Johnson were of the march on Washington and the riots.

When meetings were held, membership was often extended temporarily or permanently to the Vice-President, the Budget Director, heads of important non--Cabinet agencies, and members of the White House staff, especially one or more of the counselors.

Which has been cause and which effect is uncertain, but there is a general feeling that the individual members are less strong and able than they were when more use was made of the Cabinet as a body. To some extent, more and more they are becoming technicians or experts in their own field, but not persons of great public stature. This has weakened it even as a pluralizing factor, but the shift in the center of gravity toward the inner Presidency has been the most noticeable cause or symptom of the Cabinet's erosion. It has great need of stronger men.

Until the Nixon administration, the roles of Cabinet members as department heads were not seriously impaired. For the most part they really ran their departments unless there were special circumstances. HEW has been so large, complex, and filled with powerful subsystems in connection with Congress and its clienteles, that it almost took a superperson to handle it. When Mrs. Oveta Culp Hobby was named Secretary by Eisenhower, she found that legally she herself could select only two or three persons out of the thousands of employees. This was eventually remedied, but even by the time Robert Finch came in as Secretary, he never really got on top of it. In part, this was because he brought in an outsider as his Assistant Secretary for Administration.

Part of the difficulty here and in certain other departments such as Interior, was the reluctance of Congress to
give the Secretary a staff adequate to develop an overall
policy and program or even to monitor the ones already in
operation. This was part of the larger struggle between
Congress and the President as to which branch of the
government should control policy. It was also part of the
pluralistic subsystems, one sector of whose strength lay in
the subcommittees or committees. Out of this emanated
the legislation dealing with the powers and functions of
the bureaus and departments. One person has suggested
that each department head should have a McGeorge
Bundy of his own.[1] In this fashion he might counterbalance the viewpoints of his bureau chiefs, committed as
the latter so often were to the wishes of their clienteles. In
any event there was unanimity at the Airlie conference
that a Cabinet member should be given adequate
managerial tools on his own staff, and such subject-matter
consultants within reason as he felt he needed.

Each department chief has aiding him a number of
politically appointed Under Secretaries and Assistant
Secretaries. It is better if they are his choice, subject only
to the President's veto. However, there is a natural tendency for the White House to try to find suitable places
for key campaigners and contributors, for defeated members of Congress of his party, and also for those persons
pressed upon him by key members of Congress. It is
usually asking for trouble if those appointees feel that
they owe more to their outside sponsors than to their
department head. The best political employee is one who
is in general sympathy with the policies of the President
and his department head. Beyond this, the head will
naturally look for managerial ability and, so far as may be
practicable, for expertise. These noncareer men see themselves as change makers; conversely the career officers
under them usually resist quick change. Their ties differ.
The political appointees have their ties initially with other
politicos, often with people outside the government. The

top career men relate to each other and to the appropriations and substantive committees of Congress and their staffs, and to the affiliated professional groups outside. Loyalties also differ. The political appointees owe loyalty to the leaders above them including the President; the career men, to their agency programs and clientele, and to other career men. Career men are often older than the political appointees. Educationally they are likely to be on a par with each other.

Two very serious factors should be noted concerning these political appointees. Their turnover is very rapid. The majority stay less than two years. One-fifth last less than six months. There was a wholesale turnover after the 1972 Nixon landslide. In the second place, they come into office with little or no orientation. Any program for improvement should attack both of these problems.

Orientation at one time was provided by the old BOB. However provided, orientation should include matters such as the nature of government, its responsibilities to citizens and their needs, the roles of the Executive and Legislative branches and partnership methods between them, accountability, fairness in working with state and local units, and directives from the President.

It is clearly the prerogative of the department head to assume ultimate responsibility for the preparation and defense of his budget. In this the concept of a career man as Assistant Secretary for Administration seems to have worked out excellently in most of the instances in which it has been tried.

Formerly (and probably today with President Ford) it was assumed that the head, as either he or the President felt it necessary, could consult with the President. During the Johnson and Nixon administrations, this became less and less frequent. The White House staff performed the surrogate function in those areas which the President found less interesting or important. Almost all of the "authorities" on the subject felt that this was bad. Nixon, in setting up the Domestic Council, himself indicated an awareness of this unease, but did not follow through.

A wise President will at least ask his agency heads for ideas as to program. To aid his probing of the policies advocated by a Cabinet member, a President needs consultants on his own staff to assume an adversary position if necessary. On a more immediate level he will ask the agency heads for questions in their areas which might surface in a press conference in the offing. President Kennedy used this technique very effectively.

We are all familiar with the frequency with which these heads and their assistants are called upon to testify before Congressional hearings. Also they are usually deeply involved in more informal contacts and discussions with members of Congress and their staffs. It is at this point that candor, integrity, or the lack of one or both, make a deep impression on Congressmen. Usually career men accompany their chief to the hearings and are ready to feed him data. Sometimes the initiative for such a committee appearance rests with the department. In any event, such hearings (especially before the appropriations committees) are taken as a very serious part of the work of the chief and his assistants. They rely heavily on the corporate memory and current expertise of their senior career men, not only in preparation, but also as "backup" in the hearings themselves. Most departments now have an Assistant Secretary for Congressional Relations.

There rests also on these chiefs or their assistants considerable responsibility for service on interdepartmental committees or councils. At the top level are the Cabinet and National Security or Domestic Council meetings—or meetings of the interdepartmental committees set up by one of these bodies or the President. Where important policies are formulated, the corresponding Under Secretaries or appropriate Assistant Secretaries are often constituted a committee to carry them out.

Such dualisms permeate the government—one top-level person (usually a political appointee) for policy determination; another, just under him, political or career, to assume the management or implementation of the decision. Where the decision is important, inter-departmental, or complex, the body making the decision usually needs a staff with expertise to assist it.

Over the years certain Cabinet members have come to be regarded as the "inner" Cabinet, the ones who most share access to and consultation with the President. These are State, Defense, Treasury, Justice—interestingly enough, the earliest to be set up. The others—Health, Education, and Welfare; Housing and Urban Development; Interior; Agriculture; Commerce; Labor; Transportation—are the so-called outer Cabinet. Much more than those in the inner Cabinet, these are clientele-oriented, especially at their bureau level. This does not mean that the departments in the inner Cabinet are immune from clienteles in the pressure exerted on them. Defense has such vast contractual authority that it could never possibly be let alone by those who would profit by contract awards. From another standpoint. Justice in recent years (and probably earlier also) has been subjected to constant pressures for selective enforcement or retribution. Yet it is the outer Cabinet in which bureau and department heads are most likely to be captured by "skewed sets of personal preferences." In this sense, President Nixon's transfer of so many decisions to the White House staff was a counsel of despair. It was better after Ehrlichman and Haldeman left—better than at the time at which the first-named said that the heads of the departments and agencies, when told by the White House, "Jump," were not to ask "Why?" or "Whether," but only "How high?"

Much of what has been said concerning the departments and their heads can be said also of the independent agencies and their heads. Occasionally the head of one may be asked to sit with the Cabinet, temporarily or permanently. A few, notably the Veterans Administration, will because of the strength of their clienteles in all probability remain independent permanently. Others have been or will be absorbed into one of the departments in a reorganization.

Mostly these independent agencies are clientele-oriented, with Congressional or interest-group support. The Small Business Administration will serve as an example. But the clientele of this agency is less numerous and less powerful than has been the case with the Veterans.

The principal advantage to a President in setting up a new and independent agency lies in his lack, for one reason or another, of the necessary confidence in one of the existing departments. All recent Presidents have from time to time adopted the alternative of a new over an existing agency, for one or more of several reasons.[2]

There remain the regulatory commissions toward which the President holds an ambivalent relationship. He does appoint the members, subject to the Senate's approval, but the appointments are for fixed terms. If a President is re-elected, it does follow that eventually he can very considerably influence the orientation of a given commission through this appointive power. This holds true even though during the term of a member he cannot remove him except on grounds specified in the act setting up the commission. Recent legislation has given commission chairmen substantial administrative powers.

In theory, commissions are insulated from Presidential and other outside pressures. Yet over the years, they too tend to become clientele-oriented, in the sense that constant contact often subtly leads members to think first of that particular sector of the public they are presumed to regulate. This is extremely difficult to document, because much of the trend is part of the American business ethic that sees each industry as "serving the public." Moreover, the President—lacking removal power except for causes specified in the act establishing the commission—can do little to counteract this in the short run, even if he wishes to do so. Congress also tends to regard these commissions as at least fully as much its agent as that of the President, and here again subsystems arise.

The OMB exerts some control over the commissions for budgetary purposes, especially when the appropriate appropriations subcommittee also becomes economy-minded.

The Civil Service Commission is *sui generis*. In one sense it would be as logical to locate it in the Executive Office as it was to put the Bureau of the Budget there. However, neither the Congress nor the citizenry quite trust the President to uphold its statutory standards for the career service. President Johnson used its chairman, John Macy, as his personnel counselor, especially for key appointments. This very definitely opened up a number of the higher positions to the career men. Their tenure was usually informally safeguarded in their former or an equivalent position.

There has been considerable low-key criticism of the commission as not really adapting its procedures to the dynamic requirements of the present day. This lies for the most part outside the bounds of the Institutional Presidency, and notice is taken of it here only as indicating a potentially closer relationship.

In one sense, our present consideration of the Cabinet, the agencies, and the commissions has been introductory. It has thus far largely been a textbook presentation. The deeper dilemmas, relationships, and problems appear when we pass to a consideration of the tensions and instabilities in the many relationships involved—to the inner Presidency, to the bureaucracy, in the field of foreign policy, and finally with Congress. Here there is sharp division in both theory and practice. Here, the economic, social, and world settings reflect themselves in the changes in the Institutional Presidency. To these we next turn.

NOTES

1. See p. 58.
2. See Chapter 16 for a fuller discussion.

CHAPTER 6

Tensions and Instabilities in Relations with the Inner Presidency

In every large nation in the modern, industrialized world the expert career service is probably the major factor in determination of a departmental policy. Also probably most such expert career services are largely captives of their own past, fixed in their belief that past directions are the best. As for most of us, so for the bureaucrat. Life would be intolerable if one did not believe in one's own occupational significance, and one's own mind-sets relating to this. What really matters in such a situation is not such a belief. It is rather that the government official should either be ready to justify such a position in confrontation with his equals in competence or his superiors in authority; or be imaginative enough to modify or enlarge or even change altogether these mind-sets, if and when he is exposed to fresh and creative insights in these confrontations and otherwise.

The expert career service of the United States is no exception in such matters. The author has a sharp recollection of a hearing in which the late Senator Estes Kefauver was cross-questioning representatives of our State Department. The subject happened to be the rather far-out "Union Now" of the North Atlantic democracies. The precise issue was whether or not the United States should call an exploratory conference on the subject, with those who held to the same living democratic values. But the particular immediate and/or long-range issues are irrelevant for the point really in question. After long interchange between this Senator, whose utopia had within it the deep insights of a vaulting imagination, and the high-ranking government official, who was completely negative in presenting one argument after another as to why such a conference should not even be held, Kefauver lost his patience and blurted out, "Have you no imagination?"

This in a nutshell is the question of the "change maker" all over the world. Harry Truman and George Marshall broke through the barrier with the Marshall Plan. Whatever the motivation and however unsound (or sound) the insights advanced, the methods used, and the persons chosen to advance these insights, the overall program of the Nixon Presidency was of this character. He was trying to break through what he felt to be the established pattern in which the appointed Cabinet members so often were either taken captive by the career men or were beating their heads against the resistance of the subsystems or whirlpools of bureaus, supporting Congressional subcommittees, and functional lobbyists and clienteles in the public at large.

The argument for his side lay in part in the worldwide nature of the phenomenon, in part in the fact that every one of his recent predecessors in the Presidency had identified this same phenomenon of bureaucratic recalcitrance.

To foreshadow a later discussion of the career service,[1] the author should interject his own view (1) that more often than not the career service is sound in its advice, and (2) that in the executive training programs sponsored by our government, the elements of creative imagination and readiness to innovate are stressed, and (3) that both Congress and the political appointees of a President are themselves mixtures of vested interests and convictions of the soundness of the status quo and an open-mindedness toward the necessity of change.

Nixon's answer theoretically was to establish in the White House or the Executive Office a counterbalance in the form of a group of experts that would quarry for alternative options. His first and most spectacular success was in bringing to the White House Henry Kissinger and a corps of specialists, a few from the foreign service, a few from Defense, and a number of others. He used the National Security Council as the validating instrument for innovation in world affairs. In a sense this was no different from the Johnson task forces in domestic affairs, and the tradition consolidated by Franklin Roosevelt of establishing a new and fresh independent agency when there was a new and important job to be done. Truman with his Hoover Commissions on Governmental Reorganization and their task forces also found an instrument to plough new ground. So did the Heineman Task Force and the Ash Council.

Following the National Security Council prototype, a Domestic Council was set up by a Congressionally approved reorganization plan to perform basically in the same manner as the NSC. Associated Cabinet members could propose options of their own or filter options developed by a White House staff.

Also, individual Nixon men were inserted in each department and major agency, usually to replace counterparts appointed by his predecessors or by Nixon himself. These were expected to report to Ehrlichman and others in the White House (and usually to their agency heads as well) the extent to which and the spirit in which the agency was carrying out White House directives. To the career service—and to a considerable extent to the Nixon-appointed Cabinet member and his sub-Cabinet—these interlopers appeared as "spies," which frankly they were. There had been precedents in earlier administrations. Whether the connotation should or should not have been pejorative, as always, depends upon the point of view. In any event, the operation itself initially was fairly generally demoralizing. How far this demoralization went beyond that which normally attended a change in personnel is a matter of opinion. To the extent that these new men had direct access to Ehrlichman a new factor was added.

The Airlie House conference members and the writers on the subject were virtually unanimous in condemning such tactics—except for the theory that lay back of the Domestic Council, concerning which opinion was divided. Attention was also called to the danger of imposed standardization by agencies such as the OMB, the General Services Administration, the Civil Service Commission. Responsibility for efficiency, one participant felt, should be in the line and not in the staff agencies. A minor note was struck by a few of the conference participants usually in the form of a question, "Why did the President do this?" Was there nothing on his side? Also had there not in fact been earlier precedents at which resentment had not surfaced? The difference seems to have been in manner and in its tie-in with a downgraded Cabinet.

Without exception two other criticisms were advanced. "Arrogance" on the part of Haldeman and Ehrlichman was charged and characterized as inexcusable. Of late, a bit of the same criticism has spilled off on Kissinger. However, the real vehemence was directed at the first two, in large measure because they were deemed almost completely unqualified, either in the administrative field or in the subject content of government. Their own defense was that they were in fact Nixon's spokesmen in terms of his overall objectives. But there was plenty of thoughtful but often vehement criticism directed against Nixon himself for interposing between himself and the Cabinet and agency heads a "layer" of White House Assistants and other staff vested with authority. Incidentally these men, like Presidential assistants of earlier administrations, had never passed through the searching alembic of Senatorial confirmation.

Nor were many members of the Cabinet given the luxury of a hearing with the President himself as to either the policies imposed or the persons appointed, a situation

which was akin to the early days of the Kennedy administration, when the Cabinet had to meet on its own initiative. If the Domestic Council had had the time to become
effectively operative, this recurrent problem of Cabinets
might have been met. It was in fact one of the declared
purposes of the President when he established the council.

Plenty of columnists have attempted to read Nixon's
mind. He obviously entered the Presidency with a deep-
seated suspicion of the bureaucracy on several grounds:
(1) most of the key members dated from the administrations of his two immediate predecessors, with whose
underlying philosophies he wanted to appear to make a
clean break; (2) he feared their power over members of
his new Cabinet; and (3) he suspected that they would
work circumspectly with the leadership of the politically
hostile Congress. There was undoubtedly an advance
understanding with Secretary William P. Rogers of the
plan he (Nixon) and Kissinger had already worked out as
to the President's desire to make the great decisions on
foreign policy himself, with Rogers participating through
the NSC and in the day-to-day administration of the State
Department.

Over and above this, in many domestic matters Nixon
had relatively little active interest. Hence he limited his
contacts even with Cabinet members, whom he felt may
well have been indoctrinated with the views of career men.
In his mind they would not give him the benefit of their
own judgment but would be spokesmen for their department. He preferred on major matters to be armed with
options, and then withdraw perhaps to one of his retreats
for study and analysis, to arrive at a decision alone.

Meanwhile his immediate entourage had his ear. Evidence points to their revising or rejecting many cabinet
viewpoints—probably more than in most administrations.
John A. Volpe, Walter Hickel, and George Romney fared
especially badly. Hickel was dismissed; Romney resigned a
frustrated man; Volpe was in effect kicked upstairs.

The case of Volpe was especially interesting as reported

at Airlie. The Department of Transportation (DOT) was constantly harassed by individual, insulated White House aides. The coordinator of the President's departmental reorganization program was fed the DOT's blunders but not the interferences or the bottlenecks for which the staff under Ehrlichman had been responsible. Yet the department had succeeded in obtaining the passage of important acts such as the Airport-Airways Development Act and the Urban Mass Transportation Act. The aides never forgave DOT the compromises which had been necessary for the acts' passage, even though they were essentially in harmony with Nixon's plans. After the 1972 election these White House aides promptly got rid of the Volpe-James Beggs team and put in those who would be more subservient.

Laird as Secretary of Defense had access through the NSC; Shultz gained Nixon's confidence and access in his series of capacities. Caspar Weinberger was Nixon's man to start with, and also a first-rate analyst. Elliot Richardson was also the latter, and one who also listened with respect to the President's views. But he would not violate his commitment to the Senate concerning tenure for the Special Prosecutor in Watergate, and resigned. By then, in any event, Watergate had taken over and lay heavy on Nixon's attention and fears. The administration and the White House were grinding to a halt. Maurice Stans and John Mitchell were indicted as co-conspirators after they resigned to join CREEP.

Much of the rising tension in the Nixon administration may be summarized in a simple aphorism. "No sooner is a Cabinet member appointed than he goes off and marries the natives." A counterforce to preserve the President's objectives must be found somewhere, if options are to be preserved. Therefore the President must have independent experts at his disposal from outside the government (task forces) or in (White House staff or Executive Office staff) the inner Presidency. The problem is most acute where the whole department (e.g., Agriculture, Labor,

Commerce) is clientele-oriented, or where (like Interior) it is a conglomerate of disparate clientele-oriented bureaus. Interior has suffered, not only from its thirty or so units, but from rapid turnover among its Assistant Secretaries.

The Gordian knot may be cut at several points. A strong member of the Cabinet may be appointed who will himself institutionalize the development of options. Robert S. McNamara as Secretary of Defense was perhaps the best example. Dean Acheson was another, Mr. Dulles another. A large department like HEW may itself contain adversaries who will offer differing opinions, and a confident Secretary may report these to the President and indicate his own preference among them. The Nixon option of an expert on the White House staff has already been described. This too may be institutionalized. The top career civil service may be reshuffled, and their analytic abilities may be brought to bear upon new fields. The President may encourage confrontations in his presence, utilizing both the member of his Cabinet and differing outside *ad hoc* experts, competing Cabinet members within the government, or White House staff direction. This was the Kennedy method. A more usual alternative has been for a President either to give up the fight, believing, as is highly probable, that the career expert is right, or to establish such control as he is able via the Bureau of the Budget. In modified fashion Bundy and Walt Rostow under Johnson preceded Kissinger under Nixon in constituting themselves adversaries to those within and outside the government. Incidentally Acheson, when asked what he would have done had Bundy been brought into the White House while he (Acheson) was Secretary of State, answered, "I'd resign."

Reverting once more to the endemic, very great universal personal influence of the permanent career official, the author once studied the course in the British government of the Member of Parliament who became President of Local Government Board (later renamed the Minister of Health). For many years without exception this MP prior

to his appointment had advocated more local self-government and less centralized decision-making in Whitehall.
After his appointment to the Cabinet, again without
exception (after an interval that did not exceed six
months), he had reversed himself and was defending centralized power or advocating its increase. Such was the
persuasiveness of the key British civil servant. Interest of
the locality in its own self-government (as measured by the
percentage of the electorate voting) steadily declined
during this period.[2]

Some people have raised the question whether France
and Italy really need government other than their civil
service.

There is also no question but that one of the motivations
of the American Congress in increasing its own professional staff and in increasing the use of the Congressional
Research Service and General Accounting Office is to increase the potential effectiveness of its monitoring of the
policies of the Executive Branch.

As will appear presently, the view of the career service
at Airlie House was strongly affirmative, a view shared by
this author. Nixon and many of his appointees, like some
of his predecessors, simply did not know how to utilize it.

One problem concerns the political appointees. Under
most Presidents, as has been noted, many Assistant and
Under Secretaries of the departments have extremely
short tenure in a given office. It has already been pointed
out that the reasons for their initial appointment have
been varied, and not all of these reasons were either relevant or flattering. Nor has their orientation to their new
responsibilities been systematically approached, especially
as concerning the differences between government service and private business. Their agency heads have many
times had them thrust upon them by the White House.
Tensions accordingly multiply—between them and the
department or agency chief, between them and the career
service, even between them and the White House.

It is easy to point out the tensions and almost as easy to

recommend changes—but it was Reinhold Niebuhr who pointed out that every change, however well conceived and however much initial improvement might result, will inevitably create another set of problems. These might be derivative and secondary effects, but so long as the major decisions are likely to involve minuses as well as pluses, perfection will elude fallible human beings. This is especially true in a government as complex as ours, where any change involves a rearrangement of power, competing values, and interlocking institutions.

In other words, when we have gotten rid of objectionable people, and rearranged our institutions, there will still be problems. The inner Presidency, the department (their heads, the associates of the heads, their career men), Congress and its institutions, the press, the lobbyists, the public, the judiciary, the state and local governments—these are the major elements among which we are seeking a better balance in the assignment of powers and duties. When that new balance is achieved, there will still be rivalries, the attendant anxieties, and frustration at disappointed expectations.

Yet we must listen to the authorities, those with the most experience, those who have thought deeply. In fact, it was from this group that the Airlie conference members were chosen. They agreed that a Cabinet member should have adequate access to a President. They agreed he must assume a larger responsibility within his department and in order to do this, he must be a strong man, but not so self-assertive as to ignore the top career men. They agreed that governance must devise ways and means for options to be clearer than they now are from which the President must be able to choose. They agreed that the responsibility for choice must be shared with a strengthened Congress. They agreed that many of the Nixon tactics had created widespread unease and tension among both the earlier political appointees (especially the best of them) and the career service, and that this process undercut the public interest. They agreed that there had been a massive institutional failure.

But they also agreed that the subsystems in our government have remained for the most part untamed. They agreed that interdepartmental problems had not yet found a satisfactory method for their solution. They agreed that in many areas all recent Presidents had lost control of the government, but they also agreed that many of the persons Nixon had chosen to effect the control were especially unsuited to the task.

Nixon's organizational policies of 1972–73 were in some respects portrayed as a counsel of desperation. From the aspect of control, it has been pointed out that they involved a layering of White House political staff between the President and many of the political echelons of the departments and their career men alike. There was a wholesale replacement even among the political staff who did not conform. That the surviving White House political staff was also to be served by experts more subservient than those in the departments was a complicating factor in the attempt to run the government from the White House. A trauma of uncertainty spread through the government.

Interestingly, some Cabinet members who found it difficult to choose their own associates from outside because of White House pressure for others or White House screening, abandoned the attempt and resorted to the competitive Civil Service to fill many of their key vacancies. President Johnson at least occasionally used the same device to escape pressures from special interest.

One wonders why all this made a difference in *policy*, if Congress makes the law. This is a naive view, for many reasons. Many of the laws, under the pretense that the areas were adminstrative, actually vested whole areas of discretion with the agencies. The Forest Service never did realize that in wilderness matters Congress intentionally took back the administrative discretion it had previously granted. Also certain laws were left unenforced because of shortage of staff or denial or impoundment of funds—or selective enforcement or deliberate sabotage. There were also conflicts in laws and precedents permitting a choice by the Executive. Congress also more and more was delegating discretionary powers, while retaining right of review. The courts have left many areas as yet undefined as regards the "necessary and proper" Executive discretion. The Supreme Court, for example, has never defined the boundary between the Constitutional powers of Congress in declaring war and providing for the armed services and the President's powers as Commander in Chief. Congress has attempted to clarify roles under the recent War Powers Act in the matter of sending troops abroad. But Congress has at the same time been reluctant to prescribe regulations, even as to numbers and duties, for the White House staff. Congress is presently wrestling with this problem, and has made a foray through use of the appropriations process.

In summary, much policy is no longer statutory. The Executive Branch can in effect establish policy by manipulating organization, controlling funds, defining procedures—as well as by filling in the interstices in a given function, when the general administration has been delegated by law.

Is the real provoker of tensions the interposition of the White House and Executive Office personnel who ask questions, monitor activities, and ultimately make decisions binding on a department or agency? What does such interposition indicate? Is it (1) a goal-oriented approach by a President who must delegate powers to his staff as a practical matter, or (2) weaknesses in unequipped agency heads who have become clientele-indoctrinated, or (3) the absence of adversary procedures in the departments, or (4) an overriding need for interdepartmental cooperation which the existing structure and procedures have proved inadequate to attain, or (5) too many other claims on a President's time, so that he must delegate power to those nearest to him, or (6) too many *ad hoc* decisions in crisis situations, or (7) a chronic and basically healthy process which becomes aggravated in periods of divided government (Congress vs. the President) or when new administrations attempt to redirect old bureaucracies? Or is it all of these, and can institutional solutions be found adequate to resolve the tensions and correct the adverse factors producing them?

NOTES

1. See Chapter 8.
2. Ernest S. Griffith, *Modern Development of City Government* (Oxford, 1927), pp. 371 ff., 587.

CHAPTER 7

Foreign Policy—Whose Responsibility?

Of the awesome responsibilities faced by the American President, none looms larger, more fraught with good or evil for the nation and the world, than the decisions in foreign policy. The ultimate major decisions are the President's, subject to the instrumentalities of the Congress where required. The process of arriving at them must be institutionalized, if he is to be informed.[1]

The elements in this process, at its best, ought to have certain common characteristics. We may summarize them as follows:

(1) The options with their pros and cons should be honestly, candidly presented to the President or his designated surrogate in report form.

(2) These options should be related, not merely to the immediate situation, but also to long-range national and international goals. These goals should have been previously developed, as well as updated for the immediate problem.

(3) The principal actors in our foreign and defense establishment should have had the opportunity to participate in developing these options and goals, with or through such expert counsel as they may command and desire for the particular occasion. Such actors and counsel at the minimum should include State, Defense, Central

Intelligence, the country and area specialists in each, including the ambassadors, and (where obviously appropriate) one or more of our economic units—Treasury, CEA, Commerce, Agriculture, Labor, Transportation—and the United States Information Agency.

(4) Where feasible, members of Congress (and possibly their committee staff) should be associated with the process at one stage or another.

(5) When a decision is made, it should be communicated to the principal actors involved in its execution, along with its rationale. It then becomes binding upon all concerned in the Executive Branch and hopefully will commend itself also to Congress and the media and our allies.

Obviously, except for (1), (2), (3), considerations of temporary confidentiality in the national interest must be taken into account in the timing and extent of disclosure.

Decisions on less important matters should retain the essence of (1), (2), (3), and (5). Whether (1) should apply to the President, to the NSC as a whole, or to the head or Under Secretary of an appropriate "lead" agency, should be at the discretion of a White House Assistant for National Security. He should be kept informed of all such decisions, though he may delegate to an assistant the screening as to what should in fact reach his desk.

Whatever the body or official making the final decision on these matters, there remains the further question as to an inner consistency between *all* the goals and actions emerging from this process. I see no alternative other than the assignment of uncovering the need for some further integration or coordination either to the NSC or the White House staff or to the State Department. The NSC or the President should at least be notified routinely as to the inconsistencies discovered.

If then the person assigned in a given instance to discover such inconsistencies has been unable himself on an *ad hoc* basis to resolve them, then the matter of the responsibility for their resolution can go to either the President or the NSC and by them be either settled or debated for settlement. It would appear that the procedures outlined would maximize the values and minimize the dangers in institutionalizing the process of decision-making. All those to whom the decision was really important would be given the opportunity to participate, but not unduly to delay it. All those whose cooperation in execution of a decision is necessary would be notified in explicit terms together with its rationale. In no instance could any *one* person (except of course the President, if he so wished) gather to himself so much power as to preempt a decision by bypassing others with even a tangential concern. Remedies are provided for separating the important from the less important, but the latter would not be bypassed. All would move in orderly fashion to a decision, with deadlines set. The decisions themselves could be reviewed, if the situation changed materially or if, for example, the foreign service or one of the intelligence agencies signals the probability of a new factor entering the picture. A vehicle for a crisis or crash decision must be provided, should this be necessary. Ideally there will have been a provisional policy based on an earlier report which will be useful, but not determinative. Planning is long-range, but crises may cause revisions. Responsibilities for implementations are clearly designated, and sabotage or inertia will be detected. High morale should be maximized. Congress and the public will be kept informed, and the former can and should be given an "input" in many instances.

The procedures outlined would appear to be the best as procedures. Human frailty may abort them. They require the ablest men a President can choose, but they also require men of intellectual and moral integrity and sensitivity to their colleagues and assistants. The security of the United States and the welfare of the world deserve no less.

Having outlined these prerequisites for a statesmanlike policy decision, the experiences of the recent Presidencies will be passed in review. No one of them successfully met all of the criteria. Nixon came the nearest in his first term, and thus deserves the closest examination. The strong

Secretaries of State were Acheson, Marshall, and probably Dulles and Kissinger. All of our Presidents during this period in retrospect were "strong"; not all were equally skilled in foreign affairs or in dealing with their "team."

Especially under Acheson as Secretary of State, there was a staff attached to his office that performed something of the same function later performed by Kissinger and his staff in the White House—evaluating the memos and recommendations prepared by the specialists in State and at times emanating from the NSC, Defense, and elsewhere. It was not as systematic as the procedure designed by Nixon and Kissinger; and Acheson at times (notably during the Korean war) felt he was losing out to DOD in President Truman's decisions.

Probably never in recent years was the cooperation with Congress so close as under President Truman and Secretaries Marshall and Acheson. When the Marshall Plan was launched in broad outline and the staffs in the Executive Branch went to work on its details, there was a corresponding effort on Capitol Hill. The Legislative Reference Service lent Francis Wilcox to the Foreign Relations Committee to be its staff director and William Y. Elliott to the Herter Committee of the House in the same capacity. Each built up a staff and each was backstopped by the staff of the Legislative Reference Service. Informal cooperation among the three staffs was such that there was little or no duplication of research effort, and important material was shared. Members of both Houses visited Europe on relevant inquiries and spoke with authority on their return. The staff directors conferred constantly with their opposite numbers in the Executive Branch, not hesitating to challenge data and conclusions. Both sides sought agreement as to basic facts. Senator Vandenberg, in presenting the Marshall Plan to the Senate, said that in all his experience in Congress, he had never had such fine and thorough staff work on the part of Congress' own corps. "You can trust the findings."

When Acheson was Secretary, he and Senator

Vandenberg became close associates. Acheson would often drop in on the Senator after a hard and sometimes discouraging day, and the two would unbend to each other and take courage. The "input" of Congress in foreign policy need not be confined to the formal. This is a lesson of the Truman days to future Presidents.

To the Truman administration also belongs the creation of the National Security Council. It may, as alleged, have been the brainchild of Forrestal and James Everhart so they could poach on the State Department without saying "foreign policy." Its appropriateness lies in the inextricable relationship between defense and foreign policy.

Eisenhower was orderly in his procedures. He used the Cabinet; he used the NSC; he gave the NSC an implementing staff for its decisions in the Operations Coordinating Board; he was the first formally to appoint a White House Assistant for National Security. The "situation room" in the White House took on stature. Eisenhower had experienced both the good and the bad in United States–Soviet relations, and knew the value of Western Europe and Japan to us, and the dangers and the then necessity of the cold war.

Eisenhower relied more heavily on the NSC than did his predecessors, and there he was able to evoke real discussions. Howver, he usually allowed Dulles the last word. This "last word" was undoubtedly at times more acceptable to Defense than to State—but the cold war was our official national stance.

Kennedy was at his best in seeing the value—yes, the necessity—of introducing adversary relationships and options in policy decisions. He could move quickly in the Cuban missile crisis. He saw the need on his own staff or somewhere of someone who would have flashed a red light prior to the Bay of Pigs fiasco, and changed his procedures accordingly. He learned to recognize the need of more system in his Presidency. Like Eisenhower, he held out the olive branch of detente in his American University address, yet he recognized through his interview with Khrushchev and in the Cuba crisis that the cold war was very much a reality.

President Johnson, as the international scene became more complex with its interrelationships piling up, used the NSC as Kennedy had not. He also gave the State Department recognition as the primary instrument in foreign policy and its appropriate coordinator. Johnson relied also very much on Bundy and Rostow in the White House.

Almost certainly the military deceived Johnson as regards the Vietnam situation. For example, the author knows that one of his commanders there—not Westmoreland or Abrams—ordered the situation map altered because it showed too much territory under Communist–Viet Cong control. Granted that Johnson was not a man whose hopes one would lightly blast, this was no excuse for deliberate deceit. In general, one must recognize that no military man is ordinarily promoted for failure in his mission, whether his command is high rank or low. Rostow was also undoubtedly fed inaccurate information on the lack of progress in land reform. But Johnson really loved his country; and when he fully realized the situation, he removed himself as a divisive issue in the interest of national unity.

President Johnson made a valiant effort to give the State Department the leading role by making one of its high-ranking members the chairman of each of the various policy committees set up by the NSC and other sources. State simply did not have the capacity and perhaps the will to coordinate these committees as to policy and procedures, and Johnson's effort had to be written off as largely failing. "Wristonization"—the process of requiring all permanent key officials to serve terms overseas as well as in Washington—had produced many affirmative values in the department, but innovation and original thinking and the adversary process ("making waves") were not among them.

This brings us to the Nixon-Kissinger regime. Here our interest turns to the really great foreign policy achievements of Nixon's first term, and the procedures used to arrive at the decisions and to see that they were carried out. It is clear that the main procedural lines as well as the scale and scope of Kissinger's operations were worked out between the two prior to inauguration and probably prior to the invitation to William Rogers to become Secretary of State. Almost certainly the invitation to the latter was accompanied by Nixon's express desire himself to handle the really important decisions, and to supplement (perhaps to supersede in certain respects?) the department's staff with an enlarged White House staff under Kissinger. Rogers, through his membership in the NSC, would be kept aware of the moves in the weekly meetings, probably also aided by other direct contacts. The NSC and other channels were to be used by the Secretary for the department's input, including current matters not of hot concern to the President at the time. The two men had long been close enough friends, and Rogers was magnanimous enough, so that the Secretary was apparently ready to step aside when the Nixon-Kissinger team wanted to handle matters. This may not have helped the department's general morale, but who will quarrel with the results? It was the first White House–dominant system in foreign policy in our history. In general, the procedures were virtually similar to the ones recommended earlier in this chapter. The National Security Study Memo (NSSM) device was used, its reports stressing the emphasis of objectives rather than techniques. The NSC was a participant in the deliberations in the earlier period. The President personally made the final decisions as to options on important matters, often in one of his retreats as was his preference. These were then communicated to the NSC and to others as appropriate, and became binding as the offical objectives of the nation. They also set out the means for the next steps. However, as the months passed and the NSSM's were mostly completed, Kissinger drew to

himself more and more power. He "layered" the departments and even the NSC with a number of committees of
which he was chairman. One or another of these decided
which policies would be sent to the President for decision,
which to the NSC, which sent back for further information, which the committee itself resolved, and which
were tabled for the time being. The most important committees were the Senior Review Group, the Washington
Special Action Group made up of Assistant and Under
Secretaries (to deal with crises), and the NSC itself with
the President as chairman. This met much less frequently.
It now often served merely as a validating body. Kissinger
also chaired the Defense Policy Review Committee, the
Verification Panel, the "40 Committee" to approve clandestine policies of the CIA, and the National Security
Council Intelligence Committee. The procedure as set up
clearly marked the growing power of Kissinger, although
he and Melvin Laird clashed from time to time. Also
contact with State became less frequent, especially after
John Irwin succeeded Richardson as Under Secretary.
The same five men (with variants) were found as members
of most of six committees—Kissinger, the Under
Secretary of State, the Deputy Secretary of Defense, the
Chairman of the Joint Chiefs of Staff, the Director of the
CIA. The WSAG filled a genuine need, was innovative,
and could move quickly. Its like and its function should be
retained. Kissinger's own White House staff (which
ranged from 28 to 50-plus) was highly professional. It was
mostly drawn from State, CIA, and DOD, but with a
sprinkling from other agencies and outside. Its turnover
was fairly rapid. The staff was grouped geographically
and functionally. Its existence was largely kept from the
public, but members of the staff were encouraged to
speak out privately in their fields. They often generated
NSSM topics, established deadlines, "planned" in different time frames and levels for contingencies. The Soviet
and China initiatives were kept from the military—who
tried to find out what was going on.

Nixon and Kissinger were highly pleased with the results of their system. It permitted orchestration of various policies. The two at the top made important decisions and dominated the areas of their chief concern.

If one were to identify the most important vehicles making for success in the process indicated, they would be the Nixon-Kissinger Administration's National Security Study Memos (NSSM) and the National Security Council (NSC). For emergencies and quick decisions, the Washington Special Action Group (WSAG), established and chaired by Kissinger, shortcut the usual process. However, it did not start functioning until most of the important NSSM's were available for policy guidance. A similar body will be needed in the future, as determined by the President or the NSC.

The weakness of the system was in the neglect of areas of lesser concern to them, and in the increase in bypassing the established persons and machinery in the departments. Also, until General Alexander Haig introduced a semblance of order, there was a growing confusion in the White House group.

Whether Kissinger was effectively at one and the same time our peripatetic ambassador-at-large, our Secretary of State, and the National Security Assistant to the President remains for history to decide. It was probably too much to ask of any man, especially as there must inevitably be present the temptation to use this concentration of power to carry through his own judgments, especially as the "adversary" phase of critical sifting has, necessarily perhaps, largely been neglected. The NSC has been downgraded. When one adds to this the ever present dangers of sharp criticism or even vendettas in the press and other media as well as in some partisan circles in Congress, a unified national posture is likewise imperiled by such concentration of power.

It is popular these days to postulate a kind of paranoia in Nixon and a feeling on Kissinger's part that he had to prove his power and competence to former university associates who he believed had downgraded him. But why speculate in this fashion? Why not rather be grateful for most of the results, study the elements in the processes that "worked" to the nation's good, identify the weaknesses that came to be endemic, and plan in the future that the Institutional Presidency may avoid these weaknesses. This the author has attempted.

Some observations as to the institutions involved are in order. The role of the NSC is what a President wishes to make it. It is at its best when a President can genuinely encourage its participants to speak candidly and openly. Fortunately, both State and Defense under Kissinger and Schlesinger were headed by men of great ability and articulateness. So was the CIA, the servant of the NSC, whose function is to give its best appraisal of a given situation, preferably without a predisposed loyalty to a given option. The present Chairman of the Joint Chiefs of Staff is as yet untried. The President will be wise if he asks certain others to sit in on a given agenda, especially when economic factors are important. The new Vice-President has a rich and relevant background, and he is a statutory NSC member without departmental bias. Even on matters of cardinal importance on which an NSSM has been prepared, only the NSC and the President need be involved in the final decision.

Whether the "free-lance" staff should be in the White House (which was opposed by most of the Airlie House conferees), or on the "seventh floor" of the State Department, as under Acheson, or should relate itself direcly to the NSC, is not too important. It is important that it should be available to whomever a President may select as coordinator of the staff work of the NSC. Thus the essential objectivity would be supplied by an independence of departmental bias or vested interests. It is probably the interdepartmental coordinating role, rather than the geographic or functional specialization, that needs most staff emphasis.

Over the past decades the role of the Presidency in for-

eign affairs had been steadily enlarged. Then the claims
of almost absolute power made by Nixon clearly overshot
the mark, and hopefully this in turn has shocked Congress
and the public into a reasoned redress of separation of
powers. A measure of secrecy clearly is necessary in most
negotiations, and in the workings of a nation's intelligence
arm. Of this more later.[2] At this point one should note the
loaded dice with which the President at times rightly plays
when he claims he is privy to information not generally
available. He should not only act responsibly, but in some
fashion be held responsible. This can be in a network
within his own office, expressed through procedures that
will assure criticism; it can be in carefully chosen areas of
monitoring by a strong and responsible Congress. Leaks
to the press raise other questions, but at present public
opinion probably favors them. Public interest bodies may
be reaching the stature of the third house of Congress.

A further word should be said as to the origin and proposed content of an NSSM. It was assumed by Nixon and
Kissinger that periodically all members of the NSC would
be asked to indicate topics or problems or areas which
they believed were or might become important in our
national policy. Each topic, with a brief supporting memo,
would circulate in advance of a meeting to other members
of the council. On the agenda for each meeting would be a
decision as to whether there should be a memo, and
nominees for those to be responsible for its preparation
should be suggested. Care should be taken that State and
Defense (if it wishes) should be asked to name one of
these, but at least one additional person not then connected with either department might well be included. A
deadline for the report should be set. In general, each
NSSM should include the ultimate goal (what do we want
to see accomplished X number of years from now) and
ways and means of attaining this goal, both with options
and relevant documentation. At this stage, no recommendations were to be included. This would prevent a *de
facto* preemption of the decisions. In the first instance the

memo would be routed to a review board (a committee set up by the NSC) which should pass upon (a) its adequacy in its existing form, (b) its status requiring further consideration, (c) the level from the President down at which a policy decision should be made on it from among the options. Any NSC member (all of whom would receive copies) might ask for its inclusion on an NSC agenda. If a member felt it need not reach that level, he might attach any observations he wished to make before (c) is implemented.

The weakness in the NSSM system as instituted by Nixon and Kissinger was that, while between 1969 and 1972, 164 such NSSM's were prepared, only those deemed important at the time by one of those two men were really pressed to the decision stage where a Presidential policy and action directive issued. The machinery was too congested to do otherwise. Latin America, Africa, and the U.N. affairs were neglected. Most economic matters found their way into other channels. The procedures proposed above should remedy this. The President's National Security Assistant (or his deputy) would be charged with periodic inquiry concerning the stage that each NSSM had reached. If and when completed, in the name of the President, he would see to it that the objective of a determined goal and action in conformity with it were moving toward attainment. More than one checkup may be necessary.

The minimum essential institutional machinery as outlined is obviously full of bottlenecks, and alternative simpler modes should be devised for the issues of lesser importance to prevent clutter. For example, nothing has as yet been explicitly said as to whether a President should have on his White House staff a National Security Assistant and what his role should be. The presumption is that he should have such a person, for all recent Presidents have felt such a need. Truman might be thought of as an exception, but he really used Acheson in such a capacity. As to roles, he probably should be the one charged with screening the NSSM's, determining, under (3), which memos should reach the President's desk. Any member of the NSC might ask that it be placed on the agenda of that body. If a Nelson Rockefeller is Vice-President, he might be named to this post, or serve as chairman of a review board on the NSSM's. In this event, the review board might make the decision as to the disposition of the particular NSSM. In any case, it should be routed to the President or some person or body for final acceptability as to national policy. If it is not routed to the President, then the same person or body that made the decision should be authorized by the review board or NSC to serve as surrogate to the President in issuing the necessary directive as to our national goal. This assumes that the Secretary of State will not himself be charged with the initial screening. He may be the one chosen as the President's surrogate in connection with a given decision and may further delegate this responsibility as he wishes. So may the Secretary of Defense or the Treasury, and so on. Thus a decision on an NSSM will be made and made promptly, even though the decision is negative or deliberately deferred, with reasons given. The fact of action will in and of itself be a genuine morale-builder among those who participated in its original preparation and analysis.

The new War Powers Act is designed to limit the President's use of troops abroad which might result in another war—declared or undeclared. It demands a reporting and a rationale to Congress of each such use within 48 hours. If Congress does not approve within 60 days, the troops must be pulled out within 30 more days. The safeguards are procedural. It still may allow the President to maneuver in such a fashion that armed combat results. It leaves undefined the metes and bounds of the President's powers as Commander in Chief. The courts also are ambiguous in this regard. No one has yet successfully defined even what a "war" is.

We close with a list of major foreign policy issues likely to be with us for a long time: unities and differences in

Western Europe; the military alliance with NATO and the obligation of its various members; our relations with Japan and their relations with other nations and regions; tensions in the Middle East; our obligations to Israel and the Arabs; the oil and energy crisis, and its economic shock waves; the Cold War and the fragile detente with the Soviet Union; the beginnings in our relations with Communist China; our obligations to the Republic of China (Taiwan); future relations between the Soviet and mainland China (war, continued tension, a military alliance); Yugoslavia after Tito; armaments agreements with the Soviet; the future of Vietnam and Cambodia; anti-Americanism in Canada; the reverberations of our CIA intervention in Chile; the population explosion and consequent widespread starvation in South Asia and Africa today, and Latin America tomorrow; our attitude toward dictatorships of the right, and democracies tilting leftward, each nation being in a sense a special case; danger of a race war in southern Africa; the "new majority" in the General Assembly of the United Nations; the veto so often rendering the Security Council impotent; Cuba at our doorstep; the spread of nuclear warfare competence; terrorism by intransigent guerrillas or outlaws in search of money; recapturing good will in Latin America; great instability in international exchange; world recession; the near bankruptcy of Great Britain and Italy; double-digit inflation almost everywhere; uncontrolled multinational corporations; objectives, tactics, and adequacy of foreign aid, bilateral and multilateral; our influence in extending civil liberties, including the right freely to emigrate; extension of genuine cultural interchange of ideas; bases in the Indian Ocean; conservation of marine resources, and the development of more adequate international sea laws; pollution of international waters; the role of clandestine activities on our part.

In addition to these major crises and opportunities likely to be with us for some years, there are a number of somewhat less serious contemporary opportunities and problems requiring our attention and that of a number of other nations, including first and foremost the particular nation itself.

Cyprus; the future of Spain and Portugal; relations with Greece and Turkey; the rising power of Iran; Ethiopia; Angola; continuation of good relations with Mexico; bauxite, copper, and other raw materials with potential for cartels of nations; the Philippines; the future of Micronesia; sea power balance in the Mediterranean; Icelandic relations; Berlin.

There are a number of developing nations presently of critical importance to us and others: Indonesia, Nigeria, Ethiopia, Zaire, Pakistan, Bangladesh, India (perhaps most of all).

This list is designed to serve only as a typical "flash picture" of a given moment in time. It happens to be January, 1976. What such a list will be by the time this book is published, or three years or ten years from now is irrelevant. We may be sure there will be such a list, and that it will measure collectively the overriding importance of procedures and persons adequate to formulate our policies of national and world interest. Of such stuff is the challenge to the Institutional Presidency.

NOTES

1. Much of the detail in this chapter is based upon a paper by Chester A. Crocker, "The Nixon-Kissinger National Security Council System 1969–72," prepared for the Commission on the Organization of the Government for the Conduct of Foreign Policy.

2. Chapter 17.

CHAPTER 8

The Bureaucracy and the Career Service

Every President in recent years has complained of bureaucratic resistance or even sabotage. There must have been a reason, or a legion of reasons. Yet when one meets the senior career service, one is almost universally impressed with their ability and dedication. Somewhere there is a gulf between the Presidential generalized image and at least the potential if not the actual performance of the bureaucracy. What has gone wrong?

The problem of Presidential attitude and the danger of bureaucratic resistance are likely to be especially acute when one party succeeds the other in the Presidency. It came to a kind of climax with the accession of Richard Nixon. He could not believe that those (even the career men) who had been loyal to Lyndon Johnson's program could change their loyalties and their ways. He therefore brought with him an inborn suspicion of their parochialism and hostility. There came to be even a kind of contempt. He also brought with him a determination, which grew with his frustrations, to do something about it—to succeed where his predecessors had failed.

He was probably sound from his (and many others') standpoint in his major objectives: stress goal orientation, consolidate the clientele departments and agencies into large, goal-oriented departments, equip their secretaries with adequate staff. Group the department heads into councils and staff to deal especially with overlap. Lessen the sheer size of the federal government by transferring functions to the states and localities with revenues to match. Replace the 1,500 grants by category to these local units with broad functional special revenue sharing under a few main headings. Meanwhile step up the monitoring of the existing bureaucracy by greatly enlarging the White House staff, and placing his men in each agency. Convert the BOB to an OMB, emphasizing management. Evaluate the achievements in terms of ostensible goals of existing units, and strip down or abolish those which had not measured up. Especially when the reorganizations were complete, demand results in terms of economy and goal achievement from the department heads.

Certain of these steps have already been analyzed and evaluated,[1] others will be discussed in this chapter, and certain major objectives left till later for full discussion.[2]

The effect of the progressive unfolding of these programs upon the bureaucracy was predictable. A few here and there supported them. These were found especially among those who had the experience in management in the old BOB or elsewhere or who had been part of the creative group that helped work out one sector or another of the program. One Airlie participant said that the conference was really appalled that a President was bold enough to act out the fantasies of controlling the bureaucracy that for a long time all of the participants had vainly hoped to realize. Probably a majority of the bureaucracy dug in their heels, withdrew into their shells, and prepared themselves to "ride out the storm." Many waged guerrilla warfare and rushed to their allies in Congress and the clienteles of their agency, asked for, and often succeeded in rousing, opposition to the change. Yet "calibration and management of conflict is the core of presidential leadership," including major conflicts like this.

One must not suppose that Nixon's predecessors had

not also made efforts sometimes in some of the same directions. All confessed at least partial defeat.

Perhaps the bureaucracy does constitute the greatest threat to presidential power, but this is by no means all bad. Probably more often than not, its cumulative wisdom has headed off many a mistake. The President has various ways of learning what is going on. Kennedy, we may remember, had utilized the preparation for his press conference as one means of knowing what was going on in the agencies. Each was instructed to provide a list of current events in the particular agency concerning which he might be questioned, together with answers thereto.

Franklin D. Roosevelt made the greatest use of the most frequent major device to combat the shortcomings of bureaucracy. He simply bypassed many an established agency and created a new one for a new purpose with a fresh staff.[3] This had a not unacceptable further rationale of bringing in a vast number of patronage employees sympathetic with his New Deal. Eventually these agencies and their employees found themselves "bracketed" into the regular classified civil service.

As for the older agencies and departments, over whom a new department head and new Assistant and Under Secretaries were appointed by an incoming President, a number of different behavior patterns could follow.

Perhaps the new head was a "generalist," and brought with him little or no substantive background in the areas of an agency's concern. The top career civil servant obviously feels he knows more than his new chief, and is naturally ready to give him the agency's history, its present functions and problems as he sees them. This presentation is likely to be at one and the same time deferential and persuasive. On the other hand, the new man may well have brought with him certain White House guidelines and even warnings, but he is face to face with a man who has lived with the agency and worked his way to the top. Hence the likelihood is that he will end up its protagonist in budgetary and policy matters. This will gratify his mentor to whom such an attitude will seem altogether fitting.

On the other hand, the new chief may himself be an expert in much of the agency's concern, but with a differing point of view on some of these matters. From this point on, the future course depends much on the motivations, personalities, and style of the two men. If hopefully each has respect for the other, the new chief will explain his point of view, giving reasons therefore; the career man may and probably will raise certain questions on the basis of his experience and the agency's earlier tradition. He obviously possesses the corporate memory, and hence is indispensable at hearings and budget time. If his new chief at this point answers and calls for cooperation in the changes he proposes, he will more often than not obtain the career man's loyal cooperation, and this attitude will pass down the line. However, at one or more points resistance expressed as inertia or sabotage may show itself, and then both the strength of administrators and the loyalty of the career man will be tested. The result at such a point may ultimately depend upon the strength and expertise of the politically appointed Assistant Secretary to whom the immediate responsibility for the particular function has been assigned. If he stays on the job long enough, and is both tactful and firm, the official point of view may win out. If he leaves in less than two years, as most do, foot-dragging may defeat his chief's purpose. This is the point—or before this point is reached—at which monitoring by one of the White House staff may result in renewed assistance to and firmness on the part of the titular chief—unless the latter has meanwhile been converted to the agency's traditional course. Then the President must decide whether he, too, agrees, or becomes discouraged and surrenders, or promotes the Cabinet member to an ambassadorship, or otherwise replaces him—and the process starts all over again. Either the President or the Secretary really needs an independent staff expert as adviser who shares his views or at least develops options, to assure victory for the new viewpoint. More often than not, the more frequently people are changed, the more policy remains the same. Odds on the bureaucrat are 3 to 1 for! Which may be—as he believes —the best for the country!

This is undoubtedly an oversimplification. The new man may even find that the career man himself waited for years to see the proposed change, but was frustrated from above. In this case all may be well, unless both are overruled by impoundment or an economy wave. There are really two types of senior career men: the type that is unalterably wedded to the agency's traditional program and the type that emphasizes his skills in adapting to the new viewpoint of the new administration. This latter is ready to be completely loyal to the new. To identify this second group is more than half the battle. It will make for better understanding at this point, if we pass in review the factors which load the dice in favor of the "no change" or other view points of the first type of career man.

Some of the reasons are best expressed in contemporary satire. Parkinson's Law is a well-known and too frequent phenomenon. Under this "law" a bureaucratic unit tends to multiply procedures and "busy work" of dubious value up to whatever is necessary to keep all the existing staff occupied. It makes virtually impossible the assumption of a new function without a "survey," which probably takes time enough to kill any change. Rather than the survey, there may be a request for an additional appropriation, which may result in a jaundiced eye at any of the half-dozen stages of the appropriation process. Then there is the Peter Principle, under which each staff member is eventually promoted until he reaches his own particular level of mediocrity. There he stays, naturally resistant to any change, keeping his eye largely upon the length of the coffee break, the lunch hour, his annual and sick leave—and most of all upon the length of time which

must elapse before he can retire with his maximum
pension. Cartoons reinforce both of these images in the
popular mind.

Agencies in which these tendencies have not been
counteracted naturally tend to become "shopworn."
Promotions (not only in the State Department) go to those
who don't "make waves" which threaten the established
procedures that survive when old goals are forgotten, or
new adaptations or directions tempered by all the
comfortable berths. Nixon, in setting tasks for the new
Kissinger group, once exclaimed that he "would have to
wait twenty years for a new idea from the State Department." On the other hand, the author has most pleasant
recollections of serving under a Librarian of Congress
who demoted his Yes-men, and promoted those who
differed with him honestly.

This whole area of relationship between the career man
and the political change makers is one of the most baffling
in all governance. Certainly attitudes such as Nixon,
Parkinson, Peter, and the cartoonists expressed do not
make for creative cooperation, unless, as with some, it
stings them into thought and action, and with some others
they are willing to show their skills in carrying out a new
orientation. Distrust rarely has these positive results. If in
the end the distrust does prove warranted, subsequent full
cooperation is much less likely to result than if an initial
receptivity is assumed.

Agency rivalries are highly likely and, in fact, can be
handled constructively. Some are not so handled. For
example, there has been a notorious three-way rivalry in
water projects between the Corps of Engineers, the
Bureau of Reclamation, and the Soils Conservation Service of the Department of Agriculture. Each also had its
protagonists in Congress. Cost-benefit ratios were imagin-
atively juggled at appropriations time. The author
remembers a book written by a Navy man in the good old
days, in which he did not learn until well into the book

that the "war" referred to was not with an overseas enemy but with the Air Force!

On the other hand, at least one participant in the Airlie conference had reason to believe that the simultaneous existence of the Central Intelligence and Defense Intelligence kept each on its toes. Even the frequently differing estimates were from the very fact of their difference useful to the decision-makers. Within the Defense Department, leaks from a given branch concerning the shortcomings of a rival branch are among the most useful sources on the basis of which Congressional committees or the NSC staff monitor the entire Department. Leaks are especially useful in uncovering cost overruns or sloppy engineering by particular contractors.

Bundy complained that the Executive Branch is more nearly a collection of a hundred separate principalities, than it is a single instrument of executive action.

The relationships between the career staffs—or even the Assistant Secretaries—and the White House and Executive Office personnel almost certainly will cause a dislike of the latter by the former. It is the questions asked in monitoring that are disturbing, many of them by the OMB (BOB). These White House men obviously have a quicker time perspective—a need for speed to satisfy an impatient President. "Why so long in starting this program?" "What will it really do?" "Why so costly?" "Why haven't you collaborated with other departments?" An adversary role of this sort is both implicit and constructive.

When the question was asked of the three services, "Why don't you start an Africa program?", the Navy and Air Force said, "We'll certainly look into this important matter." The Army proudly said, "We have."

In general the White House is more successful in policy establishment, than in its follow-through.

Some agencies, and at times the White House, complain that too many checks slow up a given compliance. The insistency of the Civil Service Commission that govern-

ment-wide personnel practices be followed in recruitment
and classification is one of the most frequent excuses given
for delays. Requirements of special attention to opportunities for minorities is a worthy objective; it is also
frequently a procedural roadblock. Competitive bidding
procedures, requests from Congress or White House that
special attention be directed to favor persons, parties,
geographic areas, sex, race all may require an answer,
even if procedures are not in the end altered. A requirement of "public participation" naturally slows things
down. These are examples of the hazards to compliance
and deadlines.

One of the greatest obstacles of all and one which is the
most baffling is found in genuine conflicts of loyalty. To
whom is a given bureau actually responsible in matters of
policy, and to whom or to what is loyalty really due? The
overriding question of whether and to what extent policy
is in fact determined—by Congress or the President—will
be left to the ensuing chapter; but the dilemma of the
upper career men may be acute. For years, they may have
acted on the assumption that their meaningful policy
relations were with Congress in general and the
subcommittee in particular, out of which the authorizing
legislation first came or the funds were forthcoming or to
whom the responsibility for oversight had been assigned
by Congress. Down the line from above now comes an
order to change direction. To which body is loyalty due?
Then, too, cozy relationships have emerged with the
clienteles served, and their expectations are not lightly to
be disappointed. Moreover these career men have come to
believe deeply in the value of their work, and a rude shock
is being administered to their carefully nurtured self-
image. To the Forest Service, for example, the timber
interest and Congress are much more important than the
Secretary of Agriculture. The recreation and conservation
interest are also important, but in general they are to be
placated by a modicum of service in areas with which the
timber interests are less concerned.

Assistant Secretaries for Congressional Relations may report to the Secretary that there are Congressmen on both sides of the issue in question, and this may help opting for the position of their chief and the White House—or it may hinder it. Lines become extremely blurred, and the temptation to postpone the decision may capture the White House also. Bureaucracies and politicians alike tend to look for a consensus.

But the conflict of loyalties remains serious. The senior career man believes in the relevance of his work to the public interest. If he did not, he should resign. He is now asked to change. He was loyal to his old chief, perhaps also to a particular party. Again he is asked to change. What is his hierarchy of loyalties when there is this kind of a conflict? Or in any event is his loyalty primarily to Congress or in fact to the clientele whom his agency serves? In the event of his leaving the government, will he find alternative employment in his clientele?

Still another problem relates to his profession and his expertise. He may be asked by a new chief to do something that he believes is a step backward or perhaps plain stupid. He will try to convince his chief of the errors involved. If he fails, the temptation to drag his heels is very great. Especially this is true, if the tenure of the Assistant Secretary who is his immediate chief is likely to be short. Experience has shown that even the White House may perhaps not "follow through," its attention having been drawn elsewhere.

Sometimes he finds his chief or the White House without the supporting staff to develop plans and supporting data for an alternative. Perhaps an assist by the Appropriations Committee to the associated Congressional committee with whom he has come to work closely has deliberately kept the supervisory member of the Cabinet, without such adequate staff to supervise or develop and/or document alternatives.

Finally, he may see a number of intermediate positions formerly filled with career men of his own kind now filled with new political appointees, and again the temptation is to "handle" or convince them of the rightness of a status quo as to his own activities—or better yet have a word in his behalf or in behalf of his position spoken to the new man by a key Congressman.

Can a consensus be arrived at with the political appointees which will emasculate their newly introduced goal in return for a modest or ineffective minor face-saving alteration in his own activity?

Perhaps the agency head and political assistant have been given little discretion by the President—or his assistants—and have been denied access to the President or his staff to explain their views, and to hear the President's view firsthand. Thus their function of interpreting the agency's tradition and its problems in meeting the President's desires is blocked. Discouragement if not resignations may follow. The Secretary's ego is also hurt and his stature within the agency weakened. This is the penalty of using an intermediary, or "layering" the Secretary, if (as with Nixon) such has happened. This is also the reason for an active Domestic Council, with the Cabinet member presenting his problem. Perhaps another Cabinet member may even note an overlap, and the jurisdictional dispute, if any, be placed in a posture for solution.

The President is in a dilemma when he meets resistance within a department. For reasons already mentioned he may find it difficult to overcome. On the other hand, he may decide to deepen the layer of political appointees, filling more of the Schedule C positions (i.e., positions which allow an option in the filling) in this fashion or even tampering with hitherto career positions. This is at the price of sacrificed morale on the part of those adversely affected.

But there are remedies for the bureaucratic obstacles and tensions. Perhaps these are not complete remedies, but at least they may be ones that will release more of the potential of both the political and the career groups. Both have great potential for the public interest. This is at its maximum if they understand each other and respect the role of Congress. Though they may feel limited by this role, a substitute confidence in each other, and the maximum feasible cooperation within the intent of Congress as reflected in the law and appropriations will cement the tie. Perhaps eventually a career man, whose cooperation with his chief has been tested and proved, may be the very one someday to be made an Assistant Secretary or bureau chief. His experiences over the years with the authorization and oversight functions of Congress are invaluable.

If a new Secretary and his Assistant Secretaries would start off on the right foot, the former should meet with all the upper echelons of the career service, introduce his Assistants and their respective roles, and then very specifically indicate the President's goals for the department, his own goals under these, and ask them shortly to indicate what paths they see toward attaining them. Then, at another set time, perhaps on a succession of days he would announce a succession of meetings between each of his Assistants and those of the career service likely to be closely associated with a particular Assistant. Each should be encouraged to bring one or more other career men with him, if he felt there would be mutual benefit thereby. Each Assistant would be explaining the goals for the bureau or unit under his general direction. The career men would be encouraged to respond freely as to ways and means, and any obstacles they saw in their way. The Cabinet member himself would hold a second meeting with those concerned most directly with the overall goals as he outlined them—and at this stage he would primarily listen. This will give the career men an opportunity to tell their chief what they woud like him to fight for. At a third meeting, having meanwhile conferred with his Assistants, including especially the Assistant Secretary for Administration, he would make response, presumably meanwhile reporting to the White House as to his first two meetings and asking for revisions if any in his original instructions. By the end of the third meeting with the career men, rapport and understanding should have been established, and each group taken the other's measure. He would pledge his support to those ready to cooperate; but at the same time indicate that, while he was not looking for yes-men, he was looking for those with initiative and origin-ality in attaining the declared goals. If they anticipated opposition in any Congressional circle, he wanted to learn of it and exchange views with the Congressmen in question. He might well learn from the encounter. Most of all he wanted the long range good of the country.

On the other hand, if, as was quite probable, one or more of them might differ with the goals that the Presi-dent and he had outlined, perhaps a further individual chat might be in order. If the goal was one outlined by the President, he (the career man) might consider the possi-bility that he could be wrong—as for example, in his fear of the effects of consolidating the categorical grants under special revenue sharing. Meanwhile, would he be ready to cooperate? His tenure would be safeguarded, but not necessarily his function.

At some point, the Secretary will certainly want staff responsible to him who can deal adequately with questions raised at the expert level, and in their planning perhaps develop options. He also has in all probability the right to ask for management surveys available from OMB, in case a problem of this nature has revealed itself. If an inter-departmental problem has appeared, presumably he might raise it at the Domestic Council or directly with the other members of the Cabinet.[4] By handling matters in such fashion he will have established a reputation for promptness, and this is likely to be responded to in kind. He and his Assistant Secretaries are the link between the White House and the career service, the interpreters of each to the other. Their new environment may well not be the kind with which these political appointees have been familiar in the past, and a high-level indoctrination course suggests itself.[5]

The Secretary should consider selecting his Assistant Secretary for Administration from the career service, either from another agency or from the Federal Executive

Service hopefully to be formed someday, or possibly someone like the budget officer from his own agency who has the departmental view.

In all probability the activities of the Civil Service Commission in recruitment over the years, and in executive training, will have deposited or discovered in his agency the kind of person whom he should earmark for eventual great responsibility, if he has not already attained such a position. The agency's personnel office will gladly furnish him and his Assistant Secretaries with a list (by bureaus) of those who have gone through special training programs, including the internships in his own and other agencies. These were in all probability chosen competitively. Those who had participated in executive training programs should certainly receive invitations to the meetings with the Assistant Secretaries. The ex-interns might form a potential list for filling higher-level vacancies as they arise, or perhaps in some instances be granted educational leave for their further development. Both types of action will at once establish the fact that the hierarchy is fluid. At the same time it is interested in *persons* as such, and in their cooperation in innovation and progress in the agency's "mission."

Work should be monitored at all levels, as much to recognize good performance as to see that there is no foot-dragging. Administrative assistants of those in the top echelons will be aware of what assignments and deadlines have been set. They can simply use the telephone for such monitoring, saying that their chief was interested to know "how things were coming on." It should not be used initially, *unless there is a real reason*, as an instrument of suspicion and contempt.

Contacts with Congress should certainly be made by the political appointees. Congressmen appreciate this, especially if the attitude is "Let's compare notes." Later a request may be made—either way—and this will follow quite naturally. Each can report the upshot to the other and why.

Effective administration is not only of great value to the public concerned; it is also of great value to the department and to the public image of the President. The foregoing suggestions are of the kind that will go a long way toward assuring such effective administration. They will also uncover the noncooperators in the bureaucracy; but these will be far fewer than if the suggestions had not been followed. Each player in the game will have had his significance recognized, even though it may shift his assignment.

There are at least three other important matters making for better performance on the part of an agency's bureaucracy taken as a whole. These will be treated later in the final discussion of proposals for overall improvement in the operations of the Institutional Presidency. At this point we shall merely list them. They are: better field organization,[6] a stepping up of evaluations in terms of progress toward goal attainments,[7] and (more controversial) a drastic reduction in the size of the federal establishment, brought about by the transfer of further functions and revenues to the state and local governments.[8]

There never will be—human nature being what it is—a perfect bureaucracy. But there can be a much improved one, more responsive to a statesmanlike Institutional Presidency, and one which itself makes a major contribution to that statesmanship. However it may differ policy-wise with a given President, it must not undermine the Presidency itself.

NOTES

1. See pp. 53–57, 61.
2. See pp. 214–16.
3. See Chapter 5.
4. See Chapters 16, 18.
5. See Chapter 5.
6. See pp. 195–96.
7. See p. 205.
8. See pp. 192 ff.

CHAPTER 9

Roles in Policy Formation

By way of introduction, it may be helpful to those who are not too familiar with Congress to give a brief account of its organization, leadership, and motivations. Such familiarity is essential, if one is to understand the role of the Institutional Presidency in its Congressional relations.

The founding fathers obviously had little inkling of the complex usages that would emerge in the interrelations of the two branches. Nor probably did they visualize the great variations in these usages, variations which were by-products of the variables in the persons and tasks involved and in the times in which they lived.

They saw the President as carrying out the policies incorporated in the laws which Congress had passed. Neither substantial legislative nor judicial powers would be delegated to him by Congress. There were a few important matters specified in the Constitution which only later were seen to have major policy implications. For example, they did contemplate the delegation of a considerable number of appointments without the necessity of Senate confirmation. They did see him as the senior negotiator in foreign policy and as a Commander in Chief of the armed services in time of war. But these could readily be conceived as primarily executive. The treaty being the paramount and permanent instrument in foreign policy, its ratification by a two-thirds vote of the Senate appeared to be an adequate check on the part of the Legislative Branch. They obviously looked to his "State of the Union" messages by implication as one source of policy proposals. Through his veto power he did have very nearly the final but exceptional say as to a law, the ultimate check against hasty and ill-advised adoption of policy.

The nation has come a long way since 1787. The powerful appropriations committees often negative or modify the original authorizing legislation. Many protagonists of a strong Presidency (at least until recent events) have subconsciously or consciously denigrated Congress to a subordinate position, in large measure because Congress seemed to them so often to be parochial and obstructive. Strong Presidents have themselves discovered interstices and "implied" powers in the constitution, which they were quite ready to fill or use. We have already had occasion to describe some of these bases for enhanced policy roles for the Chief Executive.[1] While calling for Congress to be more alert to check recent abuses and usurpations of power by the President, the conferees at Airlie and the great majority of writers have still clearly been on the side of a "strong Presidency." The farthest any would go in the other direction was to call also for a "strong Congress."

What then is Congress like today?

Clearly its leadership is diffused.

There is in each house a small group in each party which, because of its positions of power, is thought of as a center of leadership. That of the majority party is obviously in the stronger position. When Sam Rayburn was House Speaker and Johnson was Senate Majority Leader, it was very strong indeed. A President, regardless of party, could in conference with these men (and their party whips, conference chairmen, and perhaps one or two others) have confidence that they could and would "deliver" on any promises they might make. Truman was especially effective in his Congressional contacts. The party leaderships are less sure or strong today, but conferences can still be productive to both sides. Often the "leadership" is itself in disagreement. However, the majority party leaderships of both Houses now meet together regularly (a recent development), and on frequent occasions that of the minority joins them. Either or both would welcome White House invitations to conference—and even under Nixon the leadership of his own party was called in from time to time. President Ford and Senator Mike Mansfield seem to have a genuine rapport.

In the House, the chairmen of the Rules and Ways and Means committees are sometimes also thought of as members of the party leadership structure.

However, the real scatter of leadership in each House is found in the rival structure which has given so much *de facto* power to committee chairmen in the fields of their committee jurisdiction. Seniority—itself an indicator of power—has assured that a committee chairman has an independent power base. Some of this rests on custom; some on formal rules of procedure adopted by the committee itself. He always has a special role as to when he calls the committee. He can at times favor in the agenda and hearings the ones on the committee that have supported him (but this more often rests on usage than on rule). He usually appoints the subcommittees. He often chooses and has first call on the professional staff. He can drag his feet by prolonging hearings or by not calling meetings. In all these matters, the committee rules usually make "revolts" possible. The chairman knows this, if he oversteps. In any event, the great majority of chairmen, who in practice have acquired and retained these special powers, have been men who have respected their colleagues, taken their wishes into account, and have not overused their prerogatives. The recent revolt in the Congress against certain committee chairmen may mark a real change in the direction of more uniformity of party viewpoint in key positions. On the other hand, it may be but a "single shot" which will have produced such bad

feeling and infighting that the old usages will reassert
themselves. The legislative function of a committee is
to determine when the time is ripe to report out a bill, and
to try to make that bill such that its report is seldom
greatly altered or defeated on the floor. The authority
that is the by-product of superior knowledge is usually an
attribute of the committee or subcommittee in a given
field—but not necessarily of the chairman. Even someone
not a member of the committee has some power. A
committee or the House as a whole will always listen with
respect—even to a freshman member who is willing to
wait his turn—if the member has really done his home-
work and speaks with the authority that comes from
mastery of a subject.

There are committees and committees in both houses.
Some are known for their thoroughness and dedication to
the public interest. Some are clientele-oriented, many
notoriously so. The former group almost invariably
secure their legislative will, especially if they are nonpartisan in their executive sessions, which a considerable
majority are. The latter group may well carry the day also;
but they must expect more attempts to amend a bill on the
floor, some of which may be successful. Some of the
amendments may come from spokesmen of opposing
clienteles, but some definitely stem from a broader view of
the public interest. The minority party may offer one or
more amendments for the record, but more often than
not a majority or substantial sector will support the bill at
final passage. Criticism is a party function, but opposition
is not.[2]

Patterns of the House and Senate are by no means
uniform in committee membership and views, or for the
body as a whole. This tends to throw most important
measures into a conference committee for resolution of
differences. The result is likely to be a compromise of one
sort or another, with (on the whole) the public interest
prevailing over the special interest. Studies have also
shown that the House of Representatives is likely to be

somewhat more successful than the Senate in having its views prevail in conferences. Its members have had more time for specialized study because of fewer committee assignments. There is also some jealousy as between committees, and this may exert a minor influence in final votes—or be decisive as to which committee is given jurisdiction in the first instance.

The Executive should also recognize certain more or less common characteristics of members of Congress because of their origins. To a considerable extent they are local in their viewpoints, or they would not be re-elected. To the President and his men this often is equated with parochialism, but he can and should see this in the aggregate as giving a massive insight into the texture of public opinion in the nation as a whole. But also there is almost always the other and frequently stronger side to a member: his love of his country and his desire—at least when it is politically practicable—to place the public or national interest first. He frequently has a civil war within himself between these two viewpoints, if they are in conflict on a given issue. His representative function, and his desire to see that his district has an experienced member after the next election, from time to time cause him to feel that he cannot vote the national interest. Yet the temperature of his vote may still make a real difference. His zeal for his original point of view may have flagged enough so that he does not try to persuade others. In the end, he may even vote his conscience and not his constituency. After all, the United States Congress is the only national legislative body of any consequence where a member may vote according to his conscience and intelligence without retribution of any consequence from his party.

What of the influence of campaign contributions and legal fees? They are made by the special interests usually to those who already support their point of view. Are minds and votes changed thereby? Whether through rationalizations or otherwise, this occurs occasionally—in *both* branches of government. It is much less frequent in Congress than popularly supposed, and recent legislation should make it still less.

Many members obtain re-election, almost without reference as to the way they vote, by the multiplicity of favors and courtesies they extend to their constituents. It may only be furnishing a high school son some information about the government, or a letter of recommendation, or straightening out some tangle related to a veteran's benefit—but the personal attention brings gratitude with it. If a member can create the image in his district of being helpful, especially if he combines this with votes in favor of some bill that advances the economy of his area, he is likely to return for many elections to come. Most members wish they could have higher standards than in fact they do, though on really important issues their conscience more likely than not rules in the public interest. What to the outsider may appear a compromise is usually the kind of brokerage that is the lifeblood of the politician at his best—the art of the possible, the recognition of elements of soundness in the opposition, the half-a-loaf that is better than no bread.

It is remarkable how Congress has institutionalized itself in so many ways that parallel the needs of the Executive Branch. The Presidency needs research staff: Congress has research facilities in its committee staffs, the Congressional Research Service (in the Library of Congress), the greatly expanded General Accounting Office, and the Office of Technology Assessment. The Executive looks to the budget services of the OMB: each House of Congress now has a Budget Committee, with a joint professional staff as well as the experienced staffs of the Joint Committee on Internal Revenue Taxation and the Appropriations Committees. The President has his Council of Economic Advisers; Congress has its Joint Economic Committee, to receive and criticize the Economic Reports from the President. The President, within limits, may impound appropriated funds: the appropriations committees (and Congress) may cut down the spending requests of the President. The President here and there has facilities for long-range planning; the Congress has its aforementioned support agencies which are designed in part to evaluate the long-range effects of proposed legislation. The Executive Branch has clientele-oriented bureaus and even clientele beachheads in agencies in the Executive Office; Congress has clientele-oriented committees and subcommittees with "incestuous" relationships with the bureaus. The Presidency has its National Security and Domestic councils to deal with overlapping jurisdictions or too blatant special interests; Congress occasionally uses tandem or fused committees and special committees to deal with similar problems, and has a dozen devices to filter out extreme demands of powerful special interests.[3] To evaluate a policy or a bureaucratic activity, the President may use a "task force;" the Congress will call on the General Accounting Office.

Thus do both branches institutionalize similar activities and meet similar policy-oriented needs.

Bicameralism, whatever else it may do (such as delay action), does go far toward assuring that in policy choices or monitoring, in one or both houses its various facilities will somewhere be used to the full.

There is one fairly serious weakness in Congress in that its committee and subcommittee structure is not integrated with the corresponding departmental and bureau structure of the Executive Branch. It has not kept pace with the changes in the latter. It is quite usual for two or more committees to monitor one subject or bureau, and to fight for jurisdiction over proposed legislation. True, at the subcommittee-bureau level, relationships often become so close that they appear more as co-conspirators than monitors. On the other hand, the jurisdiction of some committees is so fragmented that a particular Cabinet member may discover he has important relationships with six or eight committees in each house of Congress. The Bolling Committee proposals for reform of committee structure would lessen this considerably, but they do not correspond to the changes that Nixon had contemplated in his executive reorganization proposals. However, both are tabled at least for the time being.

With this much by way of background, what are the respective policy roles of the two branches? When it comes to the initiation of proposals, the division of labor is quite clear. Almost all measures that eventually become law were proposed in some fashion by one or more members of Congress long before any President included them in his program. Usually the President picks "an idea whose time has come" (or so he thinks) when he advances it in his "State of the Union" message or separately. Prior to this it is quite probable that in one form or another a number of members in each house had already introduced measures in the same field, and a first round of hearings held. Less frequently such a bill may have been reported out favorably by a committee or even passed by one house. In any event, the measure is now taken seriously by both branches; and if the President really cares about it and presses for it, it is probable that a bill on the general subject will eventually reach the floor in at least one house.

What happens at this point—or even earlier—does not follow any one pattern. A President may suffer a complete rebuff. Most often his staff contacts the committee staffs at an early stage, seeking an estimate of the bill's chances in its existing form. On the basis of these conversations, an exploration of alternative or partial measures may result, with special attention to the particular committee or house most favorable to the President's proposal. There then takes place either a bargaining between equals in power or a search for consensus which may include both House and Senate committees. Alternatively, there may be an out-and-out confrontation, with the President invoking support from the media, organized interests, or the public in general. Meanwhile he and his staff will have a clearer picture of how the key membership will be lining up, whether of his party or the opposite one. The President himself may become personally involved, working on the leadership of both parties as well as on individuals on the committees in whose hands the immediate fate of the bill lies. He has a considerable storehouse of credit, if he does not use it too often. In the end, he may have to settle for what he can obtain. Most usually cooperation comes at the committee and subcommittee level; but if the power of special interests proves too strong for the public interest as he sees it, the fight may go to the party leadership or even to the floor; or to the other house and to the conference committee. In the end, if the bill is unsatisfactory to him, he always has the veto—which is unlikely to be passed over by the necessary two-thirds vote of each house.

It is important that a President stay with his program and not let his supporters down by changing his mind in midstream beyond the point of reasonable compromise. For a while Nixon supported Daniel P. Moynihan's concept of a floor under income. Senator Abraham Ribicoff worked out a compromise with administration support which won over enough of the oppositon probably to secure passage of the bill. But Nixon pulled out the rug, and the Senator for years thereafter penalized the administration. Such a midstream change was unusual.

The Airlie conference reflected many shades of opinion as regards the appropriate legislative tactics of the Presidency. Patterns in any event will differ with persons, issues, timing, confidentiality of information, and other variables. The group was Presidentially oriented—probably too much so. It is believed that Congress should concentrate on major purposes and values. Certainly many felt that Congress seriously limited the potential of the Presidency. However, there seems to have been a receptivity to varying the pattern of negotiation according to circumstances. Sometimes the public interest is best served by bargaining out some kind of agreement between the President, Congress, the bureaucracy, and the powerful clientele or clienteles. The prevailing conference sentiment may well have been in favor of the President, at least initially, staking out a position and fighting for it. This was especially true if his position involved fighting for those otherwise powerless whose welfare was at stake. Perhaps in the end he may achieve something, with very considerable support within Congress—or both may live to fight another day when the time is more ripe for creative partnership and a constructive consensus. This whole area of the respective roles of the protagonists and cooperators in both branches of the government is extremely complex. There was a complaint voiced at Airlie that the Nixon Presidency was unwilling even to meet with Congressional committees to work out legislation. Departments themselves may make deals behind a President's back. In the end, it may involve the President and his allies in Congress fighting the powerful subsystems of the bureaucracy, the clientele subcommittees, and the special interests involved. The latter's objectives are usually a mixture of what is also in the public interest and what is not. Can the legislative process, including the Institutional Presidency, so operate as to filter out the latter and achieve the former?

There are other factors of cooperative policy formation that are less well known. For example, it is virtually automatic for a Congressional committee to send a copy of any bill which it takes seriously to the Executive Branch for its views. It may go to the President, to the OMB, or to the department most concerned—or eventually be routed to all. In any event, a committee is unlikely to take final action until the Executive makes its views known in writing or by a requested personal appearance of a high departmental official or officials at the committee hearings.

Frequently a department or bureau may—with or without the President's knowledge—do something on its own which a few years ago would at least have been cleared with the Bureau of the Budget. This is to approach a Congressman informally—or bring out in the course of a hearing before a friendly committee an incremental change which it would like to see made in the legislation presently governing its own particular bailiwick. Whatever their source—formal, informal, executive, Congressional, or clientele—perhaps numerically most laws are of this character, incremental, largely noncontroversial, the product in the first instance of a whirlpool of like-minded men in a subsystem. There are a multitude of contacts, mostly informal, in which ideas are originally spawned which find their way into a bill. If it is of any real importance, the bill must overcome the numerous hazards which beset the legislative pathway. In a particular field, even a single Congressman's will may be decisive, as Congressman John Fogarty was with much of HEW policy. The Constitution makes Congress the normal source of policy determination. Nowhere does it say the Presidency should prevail. Yet many hold this latter view, and are impatient at what they regard as the labored procedure by which Congress makes up its mind on legislation. Attention was called to the contrast with the decisiveness with which a reorganization proposal may be voted up or down. Far too many in the Executive Branch regard Congress as an institution to be "handled," or if the Attorney General can find any ground for it, however tenuous, to be bypassed altogether. These tactics make enemies out of many if not most of the Congressmen. An Assistant Secretary for Congressional Relations soon finds that complete candor is the best approach. A strong President is often strongest when he is most candid, and the public interst is also best served when Congress is also strong. It is in this combination that a consensus is likely to be the most helpful to the nation. The tactic by which the losing side tries to make the issue one of "Congress vs. the President" is stymied. The very strength of Congress is the care and time it devotes to legislation. Committee specialization plus strong staffs make this possible. A President will do well to recognize this, and work within the Constitutional checks. Nixon was even winning his fight for

budget cutting by impoundments, till scandal caught up
with him. The 1972 "mandate" brought a recklessness
which defeated him. It has occasionally been noted that
overwhelming victories at the polls have often caused a
President to be overconfident, and hence overstep the
point of Congressional tolerance. Franklin Roosevelt did
this when he attempted to pack the Supreme Court.

Anxiety was expressed at Airlie, in turn, that Congress
might overreact to Watergate, and the pendulem swing
too far in the direction of Congress blocking Presidential
policy. What was needed was a restoration of equilibrium,
such that our Constitution could function at its best.

NOTES

1. See Chapters 6,7.
2. The major roles of party are left for consideration in Chapter 13.
3. See Ernest S. Griffith and Francis R. Valeo, *Congress: Its Contemporary Role*, 5th Ed. (New York: New York University Press 1975), pp. 154 ff.

CHAPTER 10

Congress as Monitor of the Institutional Presidency

The lengthened shadow of Watergate has caused a searching of heart in many a quarter. In none has this been more true than in Congress. The Senate (Ervin) Select Committee on Campaign Activities and the hearings on impeachment by the House Judiciary Subcommittee have been the most spectacular. All over the country the eyes of people were on these two committees, and on the powers and functions of Congress in the matter. Was there no way that Constitutional checks could, have operated sooner, or no way that the monitoring of Presidential activity could have warded off even the necessity of the ultimate seriousness of the remedies?[1]

Looking to the future, can Congress be more alert without overreacting? Can the Institutional Presidency learn its lesson? The larger question of the meaning and practices of Congressional oversight in the American system of government calls for examination. In the end, it "came through" and vindicated the system.

The most thorough, normal accounting to Congress on the part of the Executive Branch takes place during the annual hearings before the appropriations committees' subcommittee hearings. The members of these subcommittees and the staff assigned to them have become genuine specialists in the inner workings of the agencies

they scrutinize. Their corporate memory is excellent—
sometimes supportive, sometimes embarrassing, always
penetrative. They often know considerably more than the
budget examiners of the OMB about an agency. Sources
available to them include leaks from the disgruntled and
the outraged. Members of Congress not even on the
Appropriations Committee are frequently sharing views
of a particular agency out of their own experience, as to
both praise and blame—or even suspicious curiosity.

The hearings are normally held in executive sessions.
They are eventually published. However, the most
searching portions often are "off the record." It is during
these periods that an agency head is taken over the coals,
knowledgeably, sincerely, competently, penetratingly.
Albert Thomas of Texas was especially good at this; John
Rooney of New York, among the most embarrassing.
Thomas used his summer vacation to visit the regional
offices. Even the Executive Office of the President is thus
examined. A degree of immunity has been extended to
the White House staff—but may not be in the future.
There has been some interest as to how many and which
were on detail from other agencies.

Certainly the agency head and his staff worry about
these hearings all the year.

Even within the committees and certainly among the
Airlie conferees, there was difference of opinion as to how
detailed these hearings should be and how rigid.
Congress, or many in it, in turn do not want Presidential
command and control too close either.

Strictly speaking, one would expect the oversight or
monitoring function of Congress would be more properly
concentrated in the substantive committees from which
has stemmed the substantive legislation authorizing an
agency's functions. Many of these committees have in fact
established special oversight subcommittees who accept
the monitoring function as a regular assignment. Other
subcommittees out of which has stemmed the relevant legislation will frequently follow up in specific instances to

see how far their original intent has been carried out. Some monitoring is usually connected with hearings on requests from an agency for further legislation and additional powers. Every so often, a public or Congressional outcry will reach a magnitude such that a committee will stage a full-dress inquiry as to an agency's performance or nonperformance of its functions. Increasingly the legislation setting up a bureau or assigning a new function will require an annual report to Congress from the committee. The abandonment of a military or naval or veterans' installation may require a committee's validation—but this is of doubtful Constitutionality.

A real problem is presented when a subcommittee and a bureau are in cahoots. Over and over again, this cozy relationship is well-nigh impenetrable and impervious to any real monitoring, save in behalf of the particular clientele which both the subcommittee and the bureau were established to serve. The recalcitrance to change is found within the bureaucracy as well as Congress. In this regard, the OMB and other parts of the inner Presidency and the appropriations subcommittee are likely to appear as allies against the common enemy of the subsystem drawn from bureau, subcommittee, and clientele. Only the Appropriations subcommittees, the government operations committees, and the White House and Executive Office are left as potential monitors to hold the bureaus accountable. In this respect, the former now have the extremely penetrating service of the GAO on request. It is often the career man who possesses the real background (rather than the political appointee) and who is more ready to respond candidly before either the authorizing or appropriations subcommittee as regards oversight. He may not agree with the congressional viewpoint, but he understands the dialogue. His tenure, after all, is protected, and in this instance coincides with the public interest. On the other hand, the Nixon White House regarded the Department of Defense as on the whole an acceptable model, whereby a comprehensive, goal-oriented department could monitor and control its separate parts. This was the basis for the Nixon recommendations for the proposed large and comprehensive goal-oriented departments. It was felt that these could effectively control their often partially conflicting clientele-serving bureaus or "administrations" in a way that the narrower existing departments had not been able to do.

Many felt that the government operations committees should play an expanded role within the Congress—that of monitoring the monitors. In other words, they should see to it that each other committee had a functioning "oversight" subcommittee. Probably this would present serious difficulties to the normal Congressional pattern of comity and reciprocity. These GO committees do have a broad statuatory responsibility over potential reorganizations which can be extended to include the inner Presidency and the more obvious duplications and jurisdictional conflicts within the agencies. If there had been a closer oversight of the White House staff, many of the abuses and excess exercise of authority under Nixon might have been called to account sooner. This committee is the one with the responsibility in each house for oversight of the Executive Office, other than of units within it which owed their authorization to other committees. On the House side, it had, in fact, asked questions concerning absence of confirmation and unavailability as witnesses (e.g., the staff of the Domestic Council). These are the types of questions on which the committee has found it difficult to press for or obtain answers.

In the Congressional Research Service and the General Accounting Office, Congress has two powerful agencies to assist it in the oversight function. While there is still a certain fuzziness in drawing a line between their activities, in general the former deals largely with analysis of legislative proposals to alter or add to existing functions, while the latter conducts primarily audits of past performances. It had always had the authorization to do this, but until relatively recently Congress had not appropriated the necessary funds for special inquiries. The GAO had occasionally turned up somewhat questionable practices or performances in its routine audit of agency accounts. Tips of these might be passed on to the government operations committees, who might then use them as a starting point of an investigation. However, the GAO now has greatly expanded staff and funds authorized for it to respond to questions by a committee (or even a single member, if staff is available) which has to do with agency performance generally, and especially in connection with costs. It is admirably suited for such a function, having the primary responsibility for auditing an agency's expenditures in any event. It is directed by the Comptroller General, who, though appointed by the President, serves for a fifteen-year term. His nomination must be confirmed by the Senate, and the law also makes it clear that he is part of the legislative establishment. Its studies thus far reveal a high order of professional competence, and have often had real teeth in them, useful to Congress in its control of Executive Branch performance. Recently it has responded to many questions concerning the White House. How much was Nixon paying for legal fees to defend himself on Watergate? How many were assigned from other agencies? How many are on the Domestic Council, and what are they working on? By and large, the White House has been responsive.

The Atomic Energy Joint Committee has always had by law and practice a very close relationship with the former Atomic Energy Commission whereby it was to be kept "fully and currently informed." It has shown that at least one Congressional committee can be trusted to keep classified information secret. Then, too, it has not only reined in the commission, as and when it felt it necessary; it has also taken its part in Congress and elsewhere, when it needed support.

The Watergate crisis has brought to the forefront not only the potential of Congress in investigating specific abuses (notably through the Senate Select Committee on

Campaign Activities chaired by Senator Sam Ervin), but also in the far more serious and unusual activity of the Subcommittee on Impeachment of the House Judiciary Committee which led to the resignation of the President. In both instances Congress demonstrated its capacity to match its responsibility with the seriousness of the issues at stake. Congressional committees of investigation will always remain as a potential central actor in any proceeding dealing with executive incompetence or malfeasance.

The more comprehensive problems associated with government secrecy and leaks will be dealt with later.[2] It should be mentioned that Congress is often the recipient of such leaks when an indignant, disgruntled, or patriotic employee believes that Congress might do something about the facts which the informant has disclosed. Congress does in fact often do something, including efforts toward remedying the situation revealed, or at least directing an inquiry toward that end.

The Airlie conference also resurrected the old chestnut of Cabinet members appearing before Congress for questioning. Not many were greatly impressed, but an interesting discussion did take place. Perhaps a new element was an indicated preference for the House rather than the Senate or a joint session, in so far as its members would be more likely to devote time and attention to the procedures. One participant advocated submitting questions in writing in advance. He felt that the confrontation would be perhaps the only way in which a bureau chief and Congress could both be made to face up to the cooperative relationship between a bureau and a subcommittee of Congress whereby the two really conspired together against policies of the Presidency and Congress alike. The use of TV for such questioning met a mixed reception. There was a covetous glance cast in the direction of the Question Hour in the British House of Commons, but the prevailing judgement was that a better result was attained by the appearances of officials before Congressional committees. The probing could be in a far greater depth.

In any event what was desired was accountability. Our system of checks and balances really provides countless opportunities for assuring this. Its only weaknesses appeared to be with reference to the powers of the President as Commander in Chief and his freedom to negotiate (and also keep secret for a while) various executive agreements with foreign powers. Both of these instruments had the potential—occasionally realized—of preempting important decisions. Also there was an extended discussion of the extent to which vital information was kept secret from Congress.[3] The question was also raised of the emergency, residual or implied power of the Presidency as claimed in extreme fashion by Nixon.

By and large, though, the heart of the genius of our governmental system was the fact that no branch could develop a center of important power long continued, which did not have to justify its conduct before its Constitutional equal. This was the ultimate restraint on an "imperial President" or an "irresponsible Congress."

By way of demonstrating the validity of this thesis, we have only to look at the battery of powers with which the Constitution and usages thereunder have bestowed upon each of the three branches in its dealing with the other two.

For our present purpose, the checks vested in the judiciary may be but briefly noted. They deal with the determination of the Constitutionality of the President's implied powers, especially in the areas of the rights of individuals, of national emergency, and of withholding of information required by Congress or the courts to perform their function. While no sharp line has been drawn as to what is or is not warranted in the way of such emergency powers, the Supreme Court ruled that President Truman's seizure of the steel industry, even during the Korean war, was not a valid exercise of such power. He might, for example, have asked Congress for authorization. Other Presidents, notably Lincoln, had used extraordinary powers, but then had often asked Congress for subsequent validation. President Johnson used the Gulf of

Tonkin resolution as validating his power in Vietnam as Commander in Chief. Actually the Supreme Court has never systematically (or otherwise) drawn a line between these powers and the power of Congress to declare war or to make rules for the provision of the armed services. As a matter of fact, it has never even defined "war."

In spite of President Nixon's earlier refusal to deliver the tapes relating to Watergate, the Supreme Court over-ruled his claim of blanket "executive privilege" in this regard, and in effect gave the power to a lower court to decide what tapes were relevant in a criminal case. Clearly the same rule would apply to proceedings relating to a President's impeachment. Other questions having to do with the extent of "executive privilege" are still unde-cided, but the judiciary's competence to make decisions has been accepted by the President. Certainly his powers do not extend to covering up illegal acts. Moreover, in the Ellsberg case, the judge saw its larger significance and used his power to protect the individual's rights.

Congressional weapons operate after the fact in the extreme case of impeachment proceedings. On the other hand, the power of appropriations is a mighty, current weapon. It can and now has been used to curtail the size of the White House staff. It can indicate displeasure with an activity even though its authorization had been granted. This has been used as a corrective in connection with specific water resource projects—although usually these had been ones which, while included in an omnibus Rivers and Harbors Act, had been opposed by the BOB. It can fix ceilings on expenditure also. Most appropriations and many authorizations must be renewed annually or on a fixed date, thus preventing a Presidential veto of the repeal of a permanent authorization. Personnel ceilings for particular agencies or functions have been set in appropriations bills. At present the President's authority to submit reorganization plans has been allowed to expire, but it will probably eventually be renewed, subject to the customary proviso in some form allowing one or both houses of Congress to veto it. This type of Congressional veto has been used in other matters also, such as trade and tariff agreements. The most recent use has been in the War Powers Act concerning notifications with reasons (48 hours) of troops overseas, and their continued presence or activity. The time limits are set in all such instances. Some still fear that a President would find ground for noncompliance. There is a tendency also to give the President power of decision over hot issues such as price and wage control—but again with a time limit. Under the Constitution there are of course the powers vested in the Senate of approval of Presidential appointments, unless specifically delegated; and the requirement of ratification of treaties by a two-thirds vote.

The question of requiring approval of Presidential appointments is now festering as regards White House and Executive Office Staff. For the present, in spite of protests and doubt as to its wisdom, such approval is now required for the Director and Deputy Director of OMB. So long as the fiction could be maintained that the members of the White House Staff were advisory only, and that they exercised no power except minor routines, the question of their approval was not raised. With the powers obviously entrusted to Haldeman, Ehrlichman, and Kissinger this question was one which sooner or later would have required an answer. Perhaps with a new President, with Kissinger confirmed as Secretary of State, and with the other two persons out of the way, the question may well be tabled for the time being. However, the logic is on the side of either depriving White House assistants of surrogate powers or requiring their confirmation, certainly if they become *de facto* Assistant Presidents. The Airlie conferees devoted considerable attention to these matters. They agreed that the White House staff should have no operating responsibility, and under these circumstances should not require confirmation. If the staff director of the Domestic Council is given power, the Council should be regarded as belonging in the Executive Office, and he should be confirmed. Many felt that the more important question was not confirmation, but who should be compelled to testify before a Congressional committee. There was reluctance to subject the White House staff to this, but it would be quite in order to require it of those in the Executive Office. In the past, Congress has been quite flexible in not objecting to the President's setting up nonstatutory committees under him and responsible to him. Truman brought the NSC in as advisory to him. Johnson abolished the National Aeronautics and Space Council, but established a substitute by executive order. There was no agreement as to who in the Executive Office should be confirmed, especially as the budget was the President's. On the other hand, its director was constantly giving orders in connection with its administration—apportionment and circulars for example. Such confirmation affects perceptions at both ends of Pennsylvania Avenue.

Congress has of late constituted agencies as giving advice to both itself and the President. As such, the heads should obviously (at least in its mind) be subject to confirmation and required to give testimony. The Council on Environmental Quality is an example. It (the CEQ) is part of the Executive Office, but is also to advise Congress.

While it did not formally add to Congressional powers vis-a-vis the Presidency, there is no doubt that the favorable image projected over TV by the Ervin Committee and the Judiciary impeachment hearings added considerably to the prestige of Congress.

There has been considerable criticism of late of the fact that Congress seems to lack a handle over the CIA and the FBI, because "intelligence" has been presumed to be protected by "executive privilege" or national security. Sentiment is undoubtedly growing for Congress to enter the area of enforcing more responsibility in these quarters. This is part of the larger problem of the metes and bounds of secrecy and will be discussed later.[4]

While it is not so relevant to the central theme of this chapter,[5] we may also pass in review the checks a President has over Congress. He is weakest in dealing with Congress-

ional roadblocks to new legislation which he deems important. He can appeal to the nation, and this may be
effective in marginal situations. On the other hand, the
President was very definitely checked through the courts
in impoundments of funds, although Congress under the
recent law may exercise the option of not insisting upon
their immediate expenditure. Nixon omitted certain items
in his later budgets which had the effect of abolishing
statutory functions. This was deeply resented, and Congress retaliated. The President's veto over legislation is his
strongest weapon. If it is overused, Congress is somewhat
more likely to muster the necessary votes to over-ride; and
also it may find other ways to show its resentment. A President can assert "executive privilege," but how far this will
be sustained by the courts is uncertain. He can also claim
emergency powers as trustee for the people. Here he is on
much more doubtful ground, unless he subsequently sub-
mits his acts for validation. He has fewer favors to grant or
withhold than he used to have—especially in patronage.
He has little to trade, and in this sense is really in a weaker
position than Congress. His chief weapons are the prestige
and visibility of position and his command of the national
networks, when he has an important message. He should
not needlessly dissipate this strength.

But Congress needs strength also. This also is best
attained by responsible exercise of its power.

Both branches can be strong; and in their strength they
can cooperate with, as well as check, each other.

NOTES

1. For the special problems involved in monitoring foreign
policy, see Chapter 7.
2. See Chapter 17.
3. See Chapter 17.
4. See pp. 178 ff.
5. See also p. 59.

CHAPTER 11

The President's Program

What do the American people expect of their President?

If one is to judge the public opinion polls as mirroring the wishful thinking when a man is first elected and then gives his inaugural, the very great majority registered of approval would indicate that the electorate (however they may have divided during the campaign) covet unity. They ask a rising above party and almost superhuman ability and leadership. They look to him to articulate national aspirations and ethical standards—and a program.

Thomas Cronin has described the textbook President as:

> (a) a strategic catalyst and central figure in our domestic and international spheres; (b) only he can be the architect of our public policy, and aggressively move the country forward; (c) a personal and moral leader, pulling the nation together, radiating confidence as he directs us to the fulfilling of the American dream; (d) if only the right man is in the White House, all will be well, and somehow whoever is in the White House is the right man.[1]

To summarize: "He is both omnipotent and moralistic-benevolent." Obviously the nation has had a Presidential

116

cult; it is fanned by the TV exposure and oversold in the campaign. The liberal-pluralist authors have overendowed his potential.

Beginning with Johnson and coming to a dragged-out climax in Nixon's second term, revision and disillusionment set in. This is in considerable danger of overshooting the mark.

Enough has been said so far in this book to permit a disentangling from the shock of Nixon's cover-up of the cover-up to examine where the textbooks have really gone astray. For one thing, White House relationships with Congress and the departments point to a sharing of the credit or blame. The myth of omnipotence is just that! Then too, in the international sphere there are other principal actors besides the United States. In domestic matters, seen in retrospect, Frankin Roosevelt's policies in many instances were seriously in opposition, one to another. Perhaps only the war saved him—or the people from disillusionment from these internal contradictions. But this is really implicit in a disparate society of conflicting pressure groups. Government inevitably suffers from this endemic economic pluralism. It is reflected in much of legislation and Congressional committee structure, and bureaucratically in what we have so often noted as clientele-oriented departments and bureaus. We look to the President as an integrating factor, the only elected official who has won a nationwide victory or mandate. Our best Presidents have genuinely claimed to be exponents of the public interest. They must not be cut back in this.

Kennedy gave the people the necessary rhetoric to commence with the right image. His death came too soon to test its validity. Eisenhower's orderliness and aloofness from the hotter partisan battles gave the people the feeling that "all is well." Only those with the leftist-liberal syndrome were aware how many were not sharing the good things of life promised by the American dream.

It was Johnson's worthy ambition to go down in history as the one who had put this right. His wars on poverty and race discrimination were genuine. He often spoke for the powerless in our society. But for Vietnam he might well have been the greatest of our domestic Presidents. He was never greater in his love of his country than when he renounced what he had hoped would have been his own future, so that somehow the nation might be united once again. Truman, after violent ups and downs in his popularity, has entered history as an authentic folk hero. As Clinton Rossiter put it, "little in little things, but gallantly great in everything that really mattered."

The Nixon program we shall leave for later analysis.[2] At this point, it is perhaps enough to say once again that he did attempt answers to the really major, endemic questions in our government and foreign relations. The tragedy was and is that somehow he appears to have substituted public relations and image for character—and it caught up with him. He was finished, not so much by the dirty tricks of his subordinates or even the reaching for power, but because he so deliberately lied to the American people, and even to his strongest supporters, except those who were caught in the same web. Traditions and values in the end meant more than organization to the people.

A President—any President—must be on constant guard against the isolation that threatens every man in a position of great power. He is also dangerously near insulation as well as isolation, unless he constantly exposes himself to Congress, the press, and his critics. In a sense, he resembles a Tudor sovereign, in the mixture of power and adulation extended him.

Of course he is expected to lead; but not so far ahead of the general public that (as Chester Bowles once said when he was Governor of Connecticut) when he looked over his shoulder, "only the League of Women Voters were following." As Theodore Roosevelt remarked of himself, he enjoyed the Presidency; it was "such a bully pulpit."

To return once again to FDR, he consciously adopted practices designed to enlist the support of Congress and the people: a broadly based Cabinet, considerable bipartisanship in appointments and attitudes, not committing himself until he had tested public opinion. The proposal to "pack" the Supreme Count was out of character.

It is interesting to speculate a bit on the probable success or failure of President Ford as a leader. Perhaps people are really ready for a leadership that is cautious with promises, and foreshadows the long, difficult paths that lie ahead in the domestic economy and world order. We shall see. He comes to office at a time of national disillusionment,with cartoonists and editors of the liberal persuasion prepared to attack with an almost chronic savagery.

What role should a President play? If we can decide this, perhaps the necessary institutional changes will appear as corollaries.

We expect our Presidents to have a program. We have also come to expect its main objectives to be set forth the beginning of each year. If at the commencement of each four-year term the inaugural address has come to hold up before the nation those broad goals, values, traditions, which have inspired and sustained us, so the "State of the Union" message has come to be the unveiling of the more concrete objectives, legislatively and administratively, which constitute a program for the year. Presently it is in three parts—the State of the Union, the Economic Report with objectives in this area following from the diagnosis therein, and the budget message, presenting in summarized form the extent of the next fiscal year's expenditures, and priorities therein with their rationale.

The entire detailed budget accompanies this message. The first message is usually delivered in person before a joint session of Congress, the others are sent to the members, with the press carrying summaries for the public at

large. From time to time the President will add other messages, as parts of his program continue to be added or am-
plified or amended. National emergencies are often made
an occasion for such a message. Occasionally there will be a
message devoted particularly to foreign policy, but more
usually this occurs in some address in an appropriate
setting.

Presidents Truman and Eisenhower regularized the
idea that the major State of the Union address should be
annual, and should follow promptly after Congress had
duly organized itself to transact business. From then on,
the media kept score on how successful a President had
been in obtaining his ends. The budget message ought
clearly to reflect the program. There is some tendency in
the case of some new departure to understate the ultimate
expenditure by the modest cost of its first year. For
example, the plans may call for its full operation to be post-
poned till well along in the fiscal year.

Once the program has been presented, the expectation is
that there will be a rising tempo of activity in its behalf on
the part of the administration.[3]

The best strategy in terms of success is probably to stake
out a relatively small number of issues, and "go public."[4]
After a new President's first year's message, he will have
much more time for preparation of programs for subsequent years, and for the occasional additions during the
year. The methods used for such preparation were the subject of considerable interest in the Airlie conference.
Sources varied with the President, but all recent Presidents
at one time or another have used the Bureau of the
Budget, the White House staff, commissions and task
forces, the CEA, and the departments and agencies—these
last-named for proposals in their respective fields. The
National Security Council has at times also been a source,
and Nixon hoped to use the Domestic Council in similar

fashion. How many items were in fact primarily traced to Congressional interest, specifically suggested and urged from that quarter, is difficult to say. Soundings may well have been taken in Congressional circles as to the probable reception of a particular idea, and the appraisal thereof a strong factor in its ultimate inclusion or exclusion. Truman used the opposition in the hostile Eightieth Congress, so as deliberately to create issues for the 1948 campaign. This was constructive combat—at the time a better strategy than to compromise, placate, or lie down. Both Presidents and Congress will turn to constructive combat, if they believe it will aid them.

When the Bureau of the Budget comprehensively performed the clearinghouse function for departmental proposals, and the successful ones were granted the coveted label, "in accord with the President's program," the bureau clearly was a major factor—not merely routine, but often creative. Probably Truman made the most use of it in this fashion.

Eisenhower's program was more incremental. As he put it, he wanted to be conservative in fiscal and administrative matters, and liberal where people were concerned. His principal sources were the departments and occasional commissions. His Commission on Intergovernmental Relations was quite good in its survey of the field, but limited in its programmatic results. Meyer Kestnbaum, its chairman, became the White House assistant on the subject, and subsequent Presidents have usually seen fit to designate at least one of their assistants to serve in a similar capacity. Eisenhower's attempt to transfer certain minor taxes to the local units was unsuccessful. The time was not ripe. Except for his final two years when he gleefully used the veto, he sought to work out compromises. The parties until these last two years were fairly evenly divided in Congress.

After 1960 the Bureau of the Budget played a less

prominent role. The center for program-building became the White House itself, aided especially in the Johnson days by a multiplicity of task forces. The task force, being less visible initially, was now preferred to a full-fledged commission. The bureau had become conservative, a restraining factor for activist Presidents. It offered the objections of the economy-minded. Also its review of departmental proposals was fairly often short-cut. Much of a President's program was now in foreign policy and the bureau was less adept or relevant in this field. Finally, under OMB, the programming was severed from management.

The White House staff has been most successful in information gathering and policy distillation. New ideas were gathered from task forces. Legislative messages were drafted, and legislative strategies designed. As regards substance, the staff tended to divide into the fields of domestic policy and legislative program, budget and economic policy, national security and foreign policy. In each of these, the impatience of the President tended to make his staff adversaries of the departments in their insistence on speed. Those dealing with budget and economic matters would also cross-question the departments on matters of costs, goals, and interdepartmental cooperation. There was also in the White House a small cadre of aides that specialized on Congressional relations. It was their function to promote the President's program, to build a consensus. The Nixon staff as a whole had its "delegate" in each department, who also searched for consensus. However, all these assistants have usually been more successful in policy formulation than in follow-through. Both Congress and the departments have built up their defenses.

The role of Bundy and Kissinger in developing foreign policy was notable. In the case of the former, the growing magnitude of his role was probably not foreseen. Secretary Rusk had not seen fit to develop a personal staff for policy formulation, and the regular machinery of the State Department was unable to generate ideas rapidly enough unless there was a crash situation. By the time Nixon and Kissinger began their strategy planning some weeks before Nixon took office, Nixon had already made his decision to move major foreign policy issues into the White House for solution. This clearly called for staff, and the "miniature state department" in the White House was the response. In the first year or two there was ample opportunity by way of the NSC for State and Defense to have an input—but eventually analysis was filtered through the Nixon-Kissinger knowhow and predispositions.

The attitude of the departments toward policy formulation was generally disappointing to the Presidents of the 1960's. The departments were excellent in their corporate memory, competent in their expertise, fairly good in voicing practical, incremental needs. They would never recommend cutbacks where they had failed in attaining goals. They were seldom innovative. When encouraged to give their own best judgment in their own or related fields, their political chiefs would usually not go beyond echoing the requests of their career officials for more money, staff, and power. This was one of the factors leading to a decision to locate more of the planning and preparation in the White House.

Both the Heineman Task Force and the Ash Council recommended under different names what came to be the Domestic Council. Both bodies were impressed with the interdepartmental character of so many of the major national problems. Both felt the White House needed better instruments for the planning that preceded program development and adoption. Both believed the President must at least institutionally involve himself in these matters. The Heineman group recommended an Office of Program Coordination for Domestic Affairs and an Office of Program Development. The Ash Council recommended a Domestic Policy Council, which would work through flexibly constituted "program committees."

Nixon's answer was to establish the Domestic Council in his "Reorganization Plan" No. 2, 1970. The functions and composition of the Council have already been noted.[5] At this point its specific functions in the development of the President's program should be noted—to assess domestic needs and define national goals, with alternative policies for reaching them; and collaborate with OMB in determining priorities for allocating available resources.

Califano, President Johnson's principal assistant in the field of domestic affairs, argued for the Council before the Senate committee—clearly demonstrating that the need for such a council transcended party lines. The Council had scarcely "shaken down," when the creeping paralysis of Watergate at least temporarily negatived most of its potential. Most of its attention has been directed to fire-fighting.

It is almost standard practice for Presidents prior to committing themselves to a particular item in a program, to "test the water." Leaks to the press that a certain policy is "under consideration" is a favorite device. It can "get the bugs out." It can also permit withdrawal without loss of face, although Ford was roundly criticized for his alleged consideration of blanket Watergate pardons. This may well have been only a newspaper canard or a rumor without foundation. An advance leak can help supporters organize; and, if the White House is seriously interested, such organization can be stimulated. It will also smoke out areas of potential opposition, and their strength can be gauged. Public participation in its formulation as well as adoption is a desirable objective in and of itself. It is likely to increase. Congress may join in this process through hearings and other mechanisms. It is an obvious advantage to obtain advance advocacy from Congressmen of both parties. A prestigious task force may be formed—perhaps with members chosen on the basis of previously expressed favorable options. Theodore Roosevelt and Hoover both used temporary, nonpolitical commissions to muster support. However, this was less effective in terms of public acceptance of its findings than if the task force had consisted of a better cross-section of informed experts and prominent at-large choices. A large national conference might be called (e.g., on the problems of the aging), which would have well known speakers and also smaller round tables to formulate or recommend separate sectors of a national policy.

With such maximum exposure, on the assumption that the response is generally favorable, the President can formally announce the result in some detail as an important part of his program. Supporters and opponents will then converge on the Congressional committees assigned the responsibility of handling the measure in the two Houses. What it will look like when the hearings are over, and the committee proceeds to mark up the bill, will soon show whether or to what extent the President has succeeded. During this entire process, White House, OMB, and the departmental aids will be busy, pushing the President's plan, bargaining if need be, and in general keeping the White House informed as to the lay of the political landscape, including details as to supporters, opponents, and the doubtful. A President is expected to stay with his program until it is adopted or defeated. Shultz and Weinberger both experienced a change of mind by Nixon in midstream.

Congress has the final word, but if the resulting bill is too far from the original target, the President may veto it. This may be what many Congressmen wished politically. The President, in course, has made known under what circumstaces and with what amendments he would sign it. This results in the introduction of a revised version, whereas many of those who had placated certain special interests with their original amendments, may now "play statesman" and vote for the new bill. This could well have been the planned tactics all along—on the part of both branches.

Ford's original program to meet the energy crisis was a clear example of the fashion in which more actors than Congress are often involved, however vital additional legislation may be as part of the total program. Much lay within the power of the Executive Branch itself. For example, renewed vigor in the enforcement of the anti-trust laws was pledged. Cooperation of the citizenry was invoked in specific conservation measures. Business was given its assigned parts, some with facilitating stimuli by the government in opening up further tracts for off-shore and continental oil exploration. Miners and mine owners were urged to step up coal production, and utilities urged to convert to coal. Congress was asked for tax incentives and for taxing excess profits, and regulatory commissions were asked to facilitate dècisions. Subsidies for developing alternative energy sources were requested. Appeals were made to citizens generally to send in suggestions. Whatever may be the individual opinion on individual items or on the program as a whole, its advance by the President was a perfect example of a President's role in attempting to lead the nation in an emergency. Congress was not convinced.

A few concluding observations may be offered on a program's content. Reorganizations within the government may be part of it, but these are not especially suited for public debate. The issues involved are too abstruse and do not lend themselves to excitement or public involvement—unless the President proposes (as Nixon did) to abolish the Department of Agriculture and scatter its functions! (He quickly withdrew this one.) On the other hand, questions of high policy do lend themselves to public discussion.

Friendly contacts at an early stage between the President and Congress are useful. Nixon lost out as he overextended his claim to "executive privilege," showed almost open contempt for Congress, and blocked access. He messed impoundment and withheld information. He used the budget process to repeal laws. He far overestimated his "mandate" of 1972. After all, in only four of the past 40 years has Congress been Republican, and Republican Presidents must learn to live with the probability that this will continue as a fact of life for some time to come.

Half of the legislative program of government is now normally in HEW. In Nixon's second term, the department's political leadership had very great difficulty in building the necessary confidence on the part of the relevant Congressional committees that the Executive leadership was even willing to meet with the committee and staff to work out possible legislation.

Policies, as has been noted in the case of the energy crisis, are to a great extent no longer statutory, and virtually out of the control of Congress in whole types of instances.[6]

Presidential leadership is usually a vital component in major matters.

NOTES

1. "The Textbook Presidency and Political Science." Paper presented at the Annual Meeting of the American Political Science Association, September, 1970.

2. See Chapter 18.

3. See Chapter 9 for methods: Chapter 13 for the role of the parties.

4. See Chapter 12 for the role of the media.

5. See pp. 26–28.

6. See Chapter 6.

Chapter 12

The Presidency and the Media[1]

From Franklin Roosevelt who used his semiweekly press conference with glee to Richard Nixon who had come to believe the press essentially hostile, and hence to be avoided as much as possible, the Presidents in between have been something of a mixture. All alike knew a conference merited careful preparation.

There was complete agreement at Airlie that a President's press conference was important and that it should be held more frequently than of late. General approval was registered of these conferences as institutionalized in the Roosevelt, Truman, Eisenhower, and Kennedy era. Some thought that the press was in fact the only effective surrogate left for the public interest.

Surprisingly, the value of the conference to the President himself was mentioned even more frequently than the value to the public. In all probability this reflected more upon the harmful effects of the Nixon semi-isolation, than upon any downgrading of the conference's primary role in public education.

Values of such conferences to the President were numerous. The questions asked and their tone brought him open windows on public opinion such as his daily digest may not have done. He could not publicly dismiss or denounce the media in general or resentful terms, as he might privately have done when he read what he considered ignorant or unfair presentations of his character or actions—such critiques to be dismissed as unworthy of his attention. Why Nixon did not hold more frequent conferences, when he was relatively good at them, is a mystery only he could clear up. His press secretary was not an effective substitute, especially when earlier statements became "inoperative." Perhaps Nixon in his second term feared the zeroing in on Watergate; while in his first term the overriding delicacy of his foreign relations might have led him to fear slips which might be disastrous. "Tilts" did not lend themselves to international amity, and might be read into even the most innocuous statements. It may be that the usual explanation was the correct one—he really did have an almost pathological shrinking from personal contacts he could not control, and cherished a visceral grudge against media in any event.

A further value to the President of such conferences has already been stressed. Preparation for them could aid a President greatly in a knowledge of what was going on in the departments and agencies, and could aid the agency heads themselves in identifying their own problems in public relations—and what the public considered important for good or evil in their operations.[2]

The press conference was a minor substitute for an ombudsman, in unearthing and securing answers to legitimate grievances or general unease in a specific area. This could include conferences with the press secretary or an agency head almost as well as with the President himself. One criticism voiced was that the White House tended to try to monopolize such conferences and did not leave enough to the departments to cause them to take public opinion more seriously. Conferences with the departments have the further advantage that the subjects would be handled by specialists. There was also criticism of the immunity from interviews (except for Kissinger) of Nixon's White House team of power-wielders.

No one doubted that these press conferences played an

important part in educating the public. Especially when televised, almost without exception they showed a President to great advantage, and his always thorough preparation gave to the nationwide audience basis for a belief that he was fully informed and master of the situation.

This brings up the question of whether or not they should be televised. Two limitations were identified—the first of which was favorable insofar as its role was public education. If the questions referred to some immediate event, the President (with the public looking on) quite logically felt it necessary to explain some of the background. This would not have been necessary in the pre-TV days, because the sophistication could be assumed of the immediate audience of reporters. Consequently the TV conference was slowed up, and less ground covered. Also the President could not limit the use of his name as the source of an answer—especially important if he had a point in the area of foreign policy he wanted to make without direct attribution. Of course, the press secretary could make the same point later, and it could be attributed to "a high government source." No one at Airlie went so far as to suggest that the President's conferences should not be televised. Their educational value probably outweighed the disadvantages, but there was a role for both types.

The Institutional Presidency must today reckon much more with the wider activity and scope of the media. This fact led to a discussion of the latter's vested interest in conflict, and of the spilling over of editorial bias into the news columns. The latter was deplored, and so to some extent was the former. However, it was remarked that news was a commodity, and conflict was exciting. One wonders whether, when conflict is lacking, the temptation to manufacture it is not sometimes too great. The picture of an administration composed of warring factions is not healthy and usually not true either, at least to the degree alleged. Sometimes conflict is very definitely educational, especially in the field of policy differences. Hence the desire that candidates for office debate each other. The incumbent usually dislikes this, partly because it adds to his opponent's name recognition, partly because virtually every officeholder has made enemies simply because his work compels him to make choices—and his opponent finds it too easy to rub salt in these old wounds. However, to refuse to debate is to disappoint, and also probably to create an impression of fear rather than adequacy.

An opinion was expressed—and denied—that the press makes up news when it hasn't enough. This was especially alleged as to the days after a big story.

The media are useful in floating trial balloons, in editorials, letters to the editor, commentators, columnists. However, the editorials calling for Nixon's resignation were seriously questioned, on the ground that resignation would result in a permanent coverup. How widely these trial balloons and other articles are dispersed and reach the public is questionable. Coverage of foreign affairs is notoriously inadquate in most of the nation. The *New York Times* and the *Washington Post* do have a few rivals in coverage, and this is good. The *Los Angeles Times* and the *Chicago Tribune* were mentioned. Incidentally the nationwide circulation of the *Wall Street Journal* was attributed to its virtual monopoly on serious journalism in whole sections of the nation. Surprising coverage was found in certain North Carolina papers and in Charleston, West Virginia. San Francisco and Boston were mentioned as deserts, but the latter (with the *Christian Science Monitor*) quite unfairly so in the opinion of this author. To classify newspapers in any event is to tread on delicate ground. Inasmuch as it was alleged that 90 percent of the newspapers in the nation supported Nixon in the 1972 election, he could hardly complain! Even among the relatively few newspapers that have Washington correspondents, there are many who are lazy and content themselves with handouts.

Newspapers came in for both praise and blame in their use of leaks. This is part of the larger problem of classified information which will be discussed at greater length later.[3]

Kennedy blamed the *New York Times* for *not* leaking the officially secret Bay of Pigs plans, believing it might have opened his eyes in time to call it off. A Stanford paper had leaked it, but the impact was minimal. Other media knew about it in advance, but held their peace. This probably caused the *Times* to reconsider its policy, inasmuch as Clifton Daniel, its editor, subsequently said that the national security, informal compact between the government and the press was wrong. You could not trust the government. Afterward, it published the classified Pentagon Papers. One participant thought someone in the paper should have gone to jail for this; others, strongly sympathizing with the anti-Vietnam point of view, believed the publication was justified. Earlier leaks connected with World War II were generally deplored, although in some instances the leaking was merely naive or ignorant. At least one instance was cited of a deliberately false leak to mislead the enemy. Wars inevitably multiply lies among high public officials, especially the military.

The press and other media are extremely sensitive to criticism. They can dish it out, but not take it. Politicians appear to be uniformly unfavorable or even hostile to the press in private, though praising them publicly. Their chief gripe is distortion in the news in the interest of sensation. The deference of politicans to the media leads the press especially to think they are statesmen and not reporters. It would be helpful if they engaged in more searching self-criticism and emerged, for example, with a defensible and consistent code as to use of classified information. The press was commended for its remarkable freedom from corruption.

The press rightly regards itself as a vehicle to campaign for reform, usually because of its exposure of abuses. This is a major role of a free press. Certainly the exposure of Watergate atrocities played by the *Washington Post* and the *New York Times* deserves the highest praise. One possible criticism is that the saturation point was overreached, and the spillover into a widespread suspicion of government and politicians generally was counterproductive.

President Truman was especially successful in utilizing the press to further his programs. Cited were the following: (1) The continuation of selective service. The *Washington Post* pushed it and also mobilized daily a number of others—the *Los Angeles Times,* the *Chicago Sun Times,* and the *New York Times.* (2) The Food for Europe program. Here Truman was joined by Hoover and Clinton Anderson (then Secretary of Agriculture) in the effort. (3) The establishment of HEW as a department. This stemmed back to the strong interest of Agnes Meyer. Katherine Lenroot had to be informed that, if she did not stop her opposition, the *Post* would train its guns on her.

Television and its commentators (except for the President's press conferences) received less attention. It was felt that, unlike the best of the press, the time factor simply did not allow treatment of news in depth. There was also the same tendency to posture among commentators that was noticeable among politicians—including Congressional committees whose hearings were televised. Addresses by the President were of key importance. In these he could set his own stage, choose his own topic for emphasis, and command prime time. Perhaps the ending of the cold war—or the beginning of the ending—dates from President Kennedy's American University address. A President can usually also be pictured in action in a favorable setting. Truman's personally guided tour of the White House was a master stroke, especially when he sat down at the piano and played a Beethoven sonata. What other President ever did or could do this!

On the other hand, the care and sense of responsibility evidenced in the recent, televised hearings of the Congressional committees dealing with Watergate and impeachment, while enhancing the image of Congress, inexorably downgraded and incriminated the President and his close associates.

Are the media ready to concede to the Presidency some degree of privacy while it is making up its mind? Can institutional confidence and integrity be maintained, if the press moves heaven, earth, and hell to secure a leak or a breach of confidence or even a rumor as to what is being discussed? What of the deliberate leak designed to preclude even the possibility of an option under consideration that might well be best in the public interest? Suppose, for example, the list of the forty defense installations which McNamara closed had been leaked *before* Congress adjourned? By withholding the announcement until after the adjournment, the move was accepted with scarcely a ripple.

Probably precise categories of what should or should not be published and when are not practicable. *Ad hoc* decisions made responsibly by persons of goodwill are the most that can be hoped for. Most persons would opt for full and early disclosure—but would grant that some (not clearly defined) exceptions would be called for. Disclosures are essential to accountability, and the spread of information technology will widen and strengthen the informed public and its demand for information.

The President is a recipient of news and editorials, as well as a producer or provocator. Each day a President usually scans a carefully prepared digest to keep him up to date. His assistant for the purpose soon learns the fields of his special interest, including the extent to which he is receptive to learning of pointed and intelligent criticism of him and his policies. If a particular medium or cartoonist never has anything good to say, there is always a temptation to omit even the most perceptive or most damaging of his emanations.

Speech writing for a President is now a fine art. Most Presidents like to have a certain style. Most want to be exciting. Most would like at least a tidbit of a new pronouncement or spark of fresh information included in each address. Several persons may well have participated in the drafting of the really important addresses. The literary historian of the future who recognized the real Woodrow Wilson from his speeches will never be quite sure of a Lyndon Johnson or Dwight Eisenhower—or any other recent President.

In all this, image building is terribly important to a President or any man in public life. He is expected, for example, to attend religious services—but this may well be more because of the symbolism it implies in our national character than necessarily a belief that it is a deep part of the President's personality. Perhaps the annual Presidential prayer breakfast and the numerous governors' similar observances are best valued in terms of the inspirational lift they give to others in these days of troubled and uncertain values. However, in evaluating the sincerity in such matters, it should be noted that neither of the weekly prayer breakfasts held in the House and Senate will ever allow either a reporter or a photographer to be present. This is to avoid any suspicion of exploitation of what is a highly personal matter.

Public opinion polls are a mixed blessing to Presidents. A strong man, such as Truman, will do what he thinks right in any event.

Perhaps being President and watching one's image does something to a person. The danger is that techniques may prevail over values. Yet many have risen to the occasion, and tried to be what people expected them to be. May their tribe increase!

NOTES

1. The discussion of the media and the Presidency at Airlie House was vigorous and perceptive. The points advanced were numerous; the conclusions were relatively few. This chapter, with exceptions noted, is necessarily, therefore, largely a rehearsal of these points—or of questions raised. Nor is literature on the subject too extensive.

2. See p. 124 above.

3. See Chapter 17.

Chapter 13

The Political Party

Today people find relatively little to discuss under the heading of the President's relations with his party. They know the party machinery has nominated him; they know he has relied in a somewhat minor fashion on this same machinery to elect him, putting it perhaps in a modest third place—behind lining up economic, public service, ethnic groups; behind massive funding of his campaign. From time to time he may lend a hand to candidates of his party in their campaigns.

People also realize he usually tries to fill his Cabinet, sub-Cabinet, and other key positions with card-carrying and contributing members of his party—but they also suspect that perhaps personal loyalty and identity with his own positions on matters relevant to the vacancy may count for more. Also he wants to recognize the various groups to which he wishes to cater, and (if he is a Franklin Roosevelt) to try to detach sectors of the rival party through appointments therefrom of key persons. Both parties try by patronage or recognition to establish beachheads, even in groups that were 90 percent on the side of the adversary in the election.

In terms of registered party membership, neither party can claim a majority of those eligible to vote. The Republicans are especially badly off in this regard. Overall, the independents plus those who, while registering as party members, split their tickets constitute the largest and certainly the decisive group in any Presidential election. This is naturally an occasion for regret on the part of those who would strengthen party loyalty.

There are two conflicting concepts of the President—as the leader of his party and as one who is attuned to the needs and desires of the entire nation. In recent years, Presidents have placed the second ahead of the first when they were in conflict. Eisenhower did say after his retirement that he wished he had done more to build up the party.

There is a lingering yearning among most political scientists and other intellectuals for two "meaningful" parties. Most of these groups being "liberals," they would like to see one party (preferably the Democrats) so constituted. Among these same groups, there is also a smaller, relatively vocal group that boasts of its "conservatism," and they believe the Republicans should purge themselves of all save those who hold their point of view. Each of these two groups would like a pairing off along these lines. The trouble is that people just will not behave in this fashion. The conservatives had their favorite candidate in Goldwater; the liberals in McGovern—and both were beaten in a landslide vote. James McGregor Burns, dropping the liberal-conservative label, favors "innovating" and "consolidating" as a basis for party division. But these labels likewise are impossible for reasons which will appear presently.

At Airlie, there were three nostalgic attempts at finding some meaningful division between the parties—in the future, if not in the present. One person called for a "strong meaningful national platform" that would bind together the President, Congress, and the Cabinet. He offered no suggestions as to content. Another asked if the various groups could make contributions to broad goals which could furnish a basis for debate between the two parties. Again there were no specifics offered. The third called for

parties based on ideas which would appeal to the intellectuals, but he confessed a complete puzzlement as to a way to
unite a beachhead in every substantial group, by some association, however vague, with its aspirations. What was it
that was said about Mussolini's methods—"To be grandly
vague is the shortest route to power; for a meaningless
noise is that which divides people least."

The party system did have a certain fairly steadfast
reality in its rival constituencies in the late nineteenth century, although occasional substantial breakaways still
occurred. There were plenty of spoils and plenty of
patronage to fight over. There was a vigorous, though
meaningless, battle of symbols, which did at that period at-
tract intense and widespread loyalties. But these methods
are now decried and outdated. There were strong local
organizations (to some extent there still are) centering in
the county courthouses and city halls. In national campaigns there were very few issues—sometimes only
one—the tariff, free silver—and parties and candidates
could fairly logically group around one side or the other
without straining conscience too much. A group of Democrats did find free silver too much for them and formally
severed their connections. Behind the scenes, there were
other economic interest group issues lurking, and there
still are today—witness the campaign contributions.
However, the 1972 campaign contributions of this
sort were more a blackmail of business by the party, than
the other way around. Incidentally, many were illegal.
Most labor union funds went to the Congressional
candidates of both parties that were favorably diposed,
rather than to the Presidential nominee. They were
mostly Democrats.

How volatile labor can be is witnessed by the fact that
Truman won 80 percent of the manual labor vote in 1948;
while the same group gave Nixon 55 percent in 1972.

There are a number of factors in the basic erosion of
meaningful party differences. Many of the great issues
today (inflation will serve as a case in point) are too complex

for parties to differ thereon. Intelligent differences sufficient to be reflected in party differences simply are not possible. Then, too, there are too many important issues, especially in foreign affairs, for all the major issues to have a cluster of positions which would, could, or should separate people on party lines. It was Senator Vandenberg who remarked, "Politics end at the water's edge." Which party would support isolationism? Which internationalism? Detente and arms limitation are laudable objectives—nondivisive—until they are concrete—but then the division is largely based upon suppositions as to the intent of the Soviet Union or China, and not on party. Both parties support close ties with Western Europe and Japan, but only the sophisticated can find issues within this orbit. Fractions of both parties enjoy the luxury of criticism of the foreigners. Members of both parties vie in their praises of Israel and Greek Cypriots. There are few Arab and Turkish constituents. But why multiply further illustrations? The number of issues is too great. Their character is too complex. The levels of education and research are too high for great clusters of points of view to split uniformly two ways. Debates go on in Congress and elsewhere but, except for the debate as to the record of the current President, they are rarely partisan.

But there are other reasons also for the erosion. Economic and ethnic issues are strongly felt, but they are mostly polarized locally and regionally. Thus they strongly influence the results of the direct primaries in both parties in a specific state or Congressional district—and usually in the same direction.[1] This localization of viewpoints is a factor in the preferential primaries and selection of delegates to the national conventions. At the same time, reform and public interest groups have lessened the power of the regular party organizations.

Disillusionment and anomie may discourage voting at all. The former may also react against an incumbent regardless of party.

Television puts the premium on the person, not the

party; and this may be one of the major factors year in and
year out weakening the party label. It lessens the power of
organization; it increases the power of financial resources.
This is the age of the candidate, not of the party. In the
end, this should be an asset to the nation—and to the party,
if the party organization can really see the importance of
nominating persons who project an image of competence,
integrity, and charisma—based on their character. As
organizations at the state and local level, they are normally
ready to rally around any victor at the primary or convention, if he bears the party label. In this sense the party is
not dead.

There is, however, a certain quality in public opinion
which in all probability plays an even greater role than any
of the foregoing factors, though it is closely related to some
of them. This is the attitude of people toward the role of
government in dealing with problems in all fields, and not
merely the economic. Broadly speaking, the voters are
divided into three groups.

One (often called "conservative" by its friends, "reac-
tionary" by its enemies) believes that government is doing
("interfering") too much, especially at the national level,
and should pause a while. Goldwater came from this sector.
Some would roll it back. Congressman H.R. Gross of Iowa
was one of these. Together, they probably make up about
25 percent of the electorate.

A second group (called "liberal" by its friends, "radical"
by its enemies) believes that, with so many serious problems
in the nation unsolved, governmental is negligent and in-
different. It should act boldly and quickly. McGovern
came from this sector. A few would go out and look for
problems. Here again, together these make up about 25
percent of the electorate.

There is another group in between—called moderate,
middle of the road, mainstream, and above all, *pragmatic*.
This group, when a problem becomes serious, believes
something should be done about it, but not necessarily all
by government, especially by the federal. First, however,

the problem should be studied—not to avoid action, but to avoid lost motion. Then, if it is clear that government has a role to play, let it play it first by going only as far as a supportive consensus will allow. Alternatively, let there first be a pilot project, to "get out the bugs." The availability of medical care to all may have reached the stage of being ripe for national action. Nixon and Kennedy would agree, though not on details. The pilot project stage in this instance was with the senior citizens and in private health care plans.

This third group probably makes up about 50 percent of the voters. Of course, there are shadings. Of course, the same person might be in group 2 on one issue; group 1 on one affecting pocket book; and group 3 in general. There are many sectional, ethnic, and economic subdivisions of this character—but the overriding mind-set is still in this third group.

What is the evidence?

Since and including 1936, both major parties have nominated their Presidential candidates from this third group, except for Goldwater and McGovern. These two were in a sense ideologues. Like Eugene McCarthy, they helped to weaken and almost destroy their party. In these two instances, by and large except for support for the loser from the hard core of the party organizers and loyalists, the voters were alienated. The other party therefore nominated and overwhelmingly elected its candidate from group 3—Johnson and Nixon. In the former instance, the candidate added the support of group 2; in the latter, of group 1—in both instances producing a landslide. Nixon in 1972 did not even have to discuss the issues concretely. His concrete issues were found in the actions he had taken and the positions assumed in his first term. Take as another example, the Eisenhower-Stevenson campaign of 1956. Concretely, only health insurance divided the two and the issue was not yet ripe. In many campaigns the noises made by the two candidates doubtless differed, but concrete differences were avoided.

Perhaps another similarity may be noted among the win-
ners. No candidate of either party since Franklin Pierce has
ever been elected unless he came from one of the top
eleven states in their number of electoral votes! Ones were
occasionally nominated, but not elected—recently,
Humphrey, McGovern, Goldwater, Landon.

The latest (1974) Congresssional campaign marked at
least a temporary collapse of Nixon's "Southern Strategy"
to line up the conservatives, to which he added a subtle
ethnic appeal. It also targeted down a large number of
incumbent "group 1" Republicans, but retained almost
every "group 3."

Congressionally, Senators like Clifford Case and
Harrison Williams, Edward Brooke and Edward Kennedy,
Ernest Hollings and Strom Thurmond, Lloyd Bentsen and
John Tower, are probably more like each other than like
the majority of their own parties in the Senate. Bentsen,
however, having Presidential ambitions, seems to be
moving out of group 1 into group 3.

Congress virtually ignores party platforms. Caucuses do
meet in both parties in both House and Senate and try for a
measure of agreement on some important bill. They are
not binding. Less and less are the majority of each party on
opposite sides on final roll calls. Percentages were as follows: 1949–1952, 54½ percent; 1957–1960, 52 percent;
1961–1964, 49½ percent; 1969–1972, 31 percent. Even in
these instances it is rare that a substantial number from
each party does not "cross over." Congressional politics are
essentially coalitions. The majority of the executive sessions, including the markup sessions of the committees, are
nonpartisan. They often reveal differences but these are
not usually along party lines. Under such circumstances, it
is not too difficult for a President from the "mainstream,"
or group 3, to build such a coalition or even a substantial
consensus whereby he can proceed in general toward the
goal he has set for himself in his program. But he must
respect Congress, and listen to its contributions to the
consensus.

It is worth noting that the paralysis which the old text-books used to predict, if Congress and the President were of opposite parties, simply no longer is the norm in a search for party positions. From 1946 to 1976, the two branches have been under different parties 16 out of the 30 years. Hence one of the underlying assumptions of the Brownlow Committee no longer exists—to the effect that the two branches would be of the same party.

These have been years of many problems, few of them dodged. If the President (as is likely) is broadly supported, pragmatic, keyed to overriding national concerns, has a few major objectives which he believes are ripe for tackling, he is likely to realize the majority of them, whatever the party in control of Congress. Vice versa, his record of vetoes on matters of Congressional initiative will not be too extensive, and the majority will be sustained. Congress and the President will bargain ahead of time so as to have an accomplishment rather than an issue—unless one or the other really believes a good fight will be good politics—which it sometimes is. Congressional-Presidential relations with Ford in the White House are a mixed bag, not yet following a clear pattern.

A President will naturally want to control his administration, and his individual appointments to particular posts are likely to be of men who share his views in the particular area, and are of his party. At times he reaches down to increase the number of partisans in Schedule C posts, and also may insist on political clearance for certain key career posts. Franklin Roosevelt and Nixon both were guilty of this latter; and in Nixon's case, because of other attitudes on his part, this proved demoralizing among many career men. In the Roosevelt administration the whole government was expanding so rapidly that there was ample room for appointment and promotion of career men. When appointments are subject to Senate confirmation, and the Senate is controlled by the opposite party, the scrutiny may be more intensive than it otherwise would be. Partisanship is quite frequently expressed by efforts to

"make the President look bad." In legislation, the opposition party may posture or offer amendments, or denounce the President's past record. The role of the party in
opposition to a President is more to criticize him than to oppose him. The role of his own party is more to see that his
views and actions have a fair hearing, than it is to support
him. Support and opposition in the end are more often
than not issue-directed than partisan. This twin function
of criticism and presentation is a valuable one, and
perhaps parties are as good an institution as any to see
that they are performed.

Other things being equal, a President will frequently use
party machinery in search of candidates for vacancies.
This frequently involves acceding to requests of members
of Congress as well as clearance prior to nominating. Partisanship may influence the conduct of the Justice Department, in the form of campaign contributions or patronage. In either case, it is inexcusable. Under the counsel of
John Macy, Johnson's White House assistant for personnel, the President made many appointments to key posts
from the career service. This was criticized by a man high
in party circles as not providing for workers in the next
campaign and as bringing in persons who did not have
"fire in their bellies." Johnson, on the other hand, defended the practice as assuring that the man had had to be
"tried by fire" to reach his stature in the bureaucracy, and
therefore was free of any hazard in scrutinizing his past
and future record.

Nixon attached great importance to personal loyalty, as
well as party standing, and this quality in him undoubtedly
led to the excesses of Ehrlichman and Haldeman as well as
to the enlightened loyalty of Moynihan. However, with few
exceptions it resulted also in competent but undistin-
guished members in his Cabinet replacements. Schlesinger
and   Weinberger   and   Richardson   were   very   able
exceptions. Kissinger was both loyal and brilliant. The
Nixon appointments of William Saxbe as Attorney General
and Ford as Vice-President were made at a time when

Nixon was himself under such fire that the tradition that Congress will confirm "one of its own" may have been a factor. This is no reflection on either man. Ford did not have to take this danger of animosity into account in his Rockefeller nomination.

A President wants to be re-elected (if eligible), or to influence the choice of his successor and secure a measure of continuity for his policies. Hence he will use the timing and nature of his administrative decisions to influence this. The same reasoning applies to off-year Congressional and gubernatorial elections, when he has a further opportunity to build a backlog of gratitude. Hopefully he wishes to reduce the normal casualties of the party in power. Nineteen seventy-four was not a normal year. If he is wise, he will try to influence the local parties to nominate the strongest possible candidates for vacancies.

Congress is 100 percent partisan in its organization of leadership and committees—even more so than some Presidents in their appointments. This partisanship does not carry over to the issues, except for the aforesaid function of criticism and presentation.

The nomination and election machinery of the Presidency and Congress is party organized and conducted. In some of the States and cities the parties may also be primarily issue-oriented, but this is the exception nationally. There is a theory that only a strong party system will give attention to the powerless. This may well be true of the ethnic crazy quilt of the boss-ridden great city. On the other hand, the civil rights proponents and opponents were from both national parties. "Access" by the powerless can be obtained through the current member of Congress, whatever his party.

The future of parties is uncertain. I see little likelihood of issues growing fewer and less complex, and relatively little likelihood of either party repeating its selection of a left-wing or a right-wing candidate for President. With the very great importance of issues in foreign relations, inflation, environment (to mention three on which neither party has a mortgage), a pragmatic dominance is probably the wave of the future with both parties, as far as the Presidency is concerned.

We repeat what we said earlier. Because of the separation of powers, which includes fixed terms for both President and Congress, the United States Congress is the only major legislative body in the world where a member may, if he wishes, vote his conscience and his intelligence without loss of party standing. We shall not lightly exchange this for the doubtful blessings of the party discipline necessary to make a parliamentary system viable.

NOTES

1. See p. 150 for results in the Senate.

Chapter 14

Pervasive Pluralism and National Goals—Conflict Resolution

"An overmighty executive is confronted with an enfeeblement of social purpose and an incoherent pluralism"—Samuel Beer.

The overmighty Executive has been tamed and driven out. With the taming and the exit have gone his proposals for remedying the "enfeeblement of social purpose and an incoherent pluralism."

Let us as far as possible disentangle ourselves from the personalities involved, and wrestle with the related problems of incoherent pluralism and enfeeblment of social purpose. In most nations, and to some extent in our own, it has been this pervasive pluralism which has struck down the social purpose. In the United States a better word than "incoherent" would be "unintegrated." It is in the direction of or within the confines of integration that social purpose must probably be found.

Pluralism is usually thought of as a multiplicity of interacting systems of power. This emphasizes its political aspect. It has another aspect as well—a variegated pattern of cultures and ethnic groups. This has always had some political by-products in our national life, since the frontier mores asserted themselves in Jacksonian democracy. In those days the problem was to overcome sectional and local disunity. With the coming of the Irish and the Germans in the mid-nineteenth century, the ethnic factor became more obvious. Today, the blacks, Chicanos, and the American Indian—especially the first-named—are learning the meaning of political power. There is still another phenomenon which is a pluralism of sorts—the various competing institutions of our government. One scholar has even named the following as implicit adversaries of the President: Congress (itself pluralized into two houses and staff), the political heads of departments, the opposition party, the high career officials, state and local governments. The President has allies as well, including sectors of most of the foregoing, and many of them fight within themselves.

In terms of governance the President has been compared to the head of an enormous conglomerate with countless subsidiaries, each with a life of its own.

When one considers the simultaneous and interrelated operation of the three types of pluralism, the question inevitably is asked, "Is the nation actually ungovernable under the democratic processes as we know them?" Suppose the groups refuse to cooperate? We must strengthen the forces leading toward the "negotiating society."

Except for the depression of the 1930s, the long period of almost interrupted increase in our GNP since the mid-1890s, disguised or muted or tempered greatly the struggle for wealth and power between the groups. Consider today the inflation, unemployment, the necessary dedication of much of our productivity to the lessening of pollution and to pensions for an increased proportion of the aged. With these hazards there is a very real question as to the possibility of evolving or reviving broadly based national goals which will serve the purposes served in the past by the "American Dream," winning the war, or even material growth in the per capita GNP.

Apart from the increasingly tenuous influence of political party, there are three principal origins of decision-making in our government. The first of these is the interest group itself. An enormously complicating factor is the effect, especially upon the various economic groups, of technological and social separation and of the extent to which everybody from Adam Smith to the local Rotary Club has taught each of these groups to identify its prosperity with the general welfare. This gives a rationale to their efforts to use government for the purpose. A further complication is the fact that so many of the hitherto relatively powerless groups, especially the ethnic minorities, seek an instant equality, not merely of opportunity, but of income and status. It does not indicate a lack of either understanding or sympathetic cooperation with these groups to point out the historic fact that the path out of ethnic enclaves in the cities in the past usually involved a span of about fifty years or till the third generation. This was shortened somewhat in the case of the Jews, perhaps required a bit longer with the French Canadians, but they both, along with the Irish, the Germans, the Scandinavians, the Italians, the Greeks, the Slavs, the Chinese, and Japanese, have now "made it" in terms of income, political power and officeholding, and social acceptability. These latter values have come more and more to be based on their occupational and educational status rather than their ethnic character. The one exception to date of the urban dwellers to this fifty-year phenomenon has been the Chicanos. Even these might perhaps find a parallel in the French Canadians in their somewhat delayed participation in political activity and educational ambition. The blacks whose *urban* domicile dates only from World War I, and then only fractionally, are now demonstrating the same capacities. Those who remained longer in the rural South have not yet begun their "fifty years." The Puerto Ricans are relatively new arrivals.

Justice requires that none should wait who are ready and willing to work hard for an education, but sociological and environmental factors remain major handicaps still for millions of the children. To some extent, organized political clout on the part of the ethnic group itself can speed the process.

Yet we are proud of our economic pluralism, and rightly so. In economic pluralism, "what is good for General Motors is good for the country"—most of the time. The function of government is to cooperate with the good, often by nonintervention, and somehow filter out the bad. In the vitality of these economic groups lies the principal cause of the highest standard of living in the world. Yet the recent spiraling "stagflation" and the rash of "administered" prices raise serious questions of whether or to what extent the aforesaid filters may not be greatly needed. Or are we in the middle of macroeconomic forces which need government intervention? We await the President's leadership.

We should be proud also of our cultural pluralism, for it enlarges greatly the possibilities of a rich and rare cultural tapestry in our society.

Yet students of our government have not hesitated to point out that these pluralisms, when they take the form (as they usually do) of organized political groups, have come to be the most powerful single factor in our decision-making. Fortunately, the "brokerage" of the politicians, including the President, may be greatly strengthened thereby. Consumers, environmental, conservation, most educational and public health groups, are looking toward the welfare of future generations as well as toward a better present.

These pluralisms have figured considerably in the earlier chapters, and they will appear later also. We noted them in the bureaucracy and its clientele and Congressional subcommittee relationships, in the Congress, in Presidential appointments, in campaign financing, in their representation in the Executive Office. They surfaced in foreign policy, in Presidents' programs, in the political parties and coalition politics—to mention a few. Hence the term "pervasive," and its great power to undermine national goals.

To say that the three principal pressure groups—each reflected in the department—are agriculture, commerce, and labor—is to oversimplify. Each of these is divided many times over—agriculture by commodities, commerce by rival industries and rivalries between exporters and importers, labor by its various unions—to mention some of the most obvious. Each of the major professions has a lobby, although the clergy generally lobbies for "good causes."

The more recent departments—HEW, Transportation, HUD—are more goal-oriented and the interest-group rivalry is substantially *within* each and more or less settled there. They and DOD ideally furnish models for even more comprehensive future goal-oriented departments—but their separate bureaus (like those of the Department of the Interior) will be centers of the triumvirates making up the whirlpool-generated legislation.[1]

Opinion at Airlie differed as to the extent of the "ganging up" by these subsystems. All agreed it was a problem.

Some political scientists tend to write as though they thought that interest-group brokerage was all there was to the activities of the Presidency (and especially) Congress. "Trade-off" is the expression of this in contemporary vocabulary, and countervailing abuses their only hope. But there is a public interest which is quite different from adding together the demands of the economic pressure groups, or establishing a labor-agriculture alliance. Conflict management is an inevitable and major part of a President's statesmanship. But such management ought to require the injection of a public interest component, or at the very least a filtering out of the generally harmful, over and above the bargaining and compromise between warring economic groups. The goals of a clean environment and energy conservation require the President and Congress to resolve some conflicts in the interest of generations yet unborn.

So the second great source of decisions in government is, or should be, from those persons or agencies that have this public-interest integrating function. This is at the heart of the desire of many that White House and

Congress alike should have at their disposal an agency or agencies prepared to research for and perhaps even dramatize the long-range consequences of existing and proposed measures, or to plan for measures not yet known. But then the dramatization might better be left to the President, a political party, or Congress—so that the planning agency would have a chance to survive! It will have to confront many a powerful special interest, as the Environmental Protection Agency already knows.

It is here that important overriding national goals are needed, which can capture the imagination and command the support of a majority of the public. What will these goals be? The Club of Rome says they must include survival of the human species. The United Nations says that this must include the abolition of war. In the past our people have rallied to the standard of equality of opportunity for all—the American Dream. City planning says, "Make no little plans. They have no magic to stir men's souls." The Great Society, the New Deal were calls to battle, and not mere slogans—however much their concrete expression fell short of its promise. Because of shortfalls of this type, rhetoric is at a discount.

Britain is today asked by its Labour Party to rally to a new "Social Contract." The miners were the first to refuse. Kennedy's inaugural was a call to a peacetime battle; but then he failed to give any marching orders. We ourselves are indulging in rhetoric at this point—but the rhetoric still awaits a blueprint that will ring as true as its slogans. Then will come the real test for our pluralism.

The dilemma a President thus faces was illustrated by President Johnson's valiant attempts. He confronted the weaknesses in bureaucratic, clientele-oriented analyses by a series of forty-five task forces. As their reports and recommendations poured in, he turned them over to the Bureau of the Budget and Califano's office meetings for analysis. The BOB was directed to hold the line on expenditure; Califano, to develop the President's program in positive and political terms. Time ran out before the two could integrate their results. The BOB hadn't finished and Califano had had to answer 5,000 questions a day on current matters. One more year might have effected the integration.

Planning itself would be but one facet of a third and increasingly powerful strand in decision-making. This is the research and scientific approach. An agency is often tempted to determine its conclusions before its research, and to make the latter an arm of the case to increase its power, size, and clientele service. Here is one case for independent evaluations—for the potential of the GAO, the CRS, the task force, a Brookings contract, a long-range planning unit, the Congressional Office of Technology Assessment. Congress and the Presidency have only just begun to grapple with this particular problem, although billions are spent annually on government research. Evaluations and advance planning without departmental bias can be defended in part by the fact that so many problems cut across departmental lines.

The Presidency is at its best when it formulates programs in the light of the integrating factor and the research findings. But so much of the problem remains political. This political approach must be taken into account, for it may well have the last word.

The mutual support given a policy by a bureau, its clientele, and the corresponding Congressional subcommittee cannot help but subtly indoctrinate an agency head, or even the higher-ups in the Presidency and Congressional leadership. With the allegation that these relationships constitute a veritable cabal, went the extreme suggestion that the career service simply not be allowed to appear before the Congressional committees.

In the regulatory commissions and the military, something of the same process goes on. Each relevant special interest seeks to have its supporters in key positions, especially those Presidentially appointed. Where a commission or a department is charged with arbitrating between two or more groups, the President may try to have them all represented, or he may turn to public-spirited, research-oriented neutrals. Use of the two-hatted White House staff was an attempt in part to foil the bureaucracy by making some of its heads more accessible to Presidential impact. Congress is ambivalent. On the one hand, its perception of its policy function undermines Presidential control. Yet it also looks to him for leadership, and may pass on to him the really hot issues such as gas rationing or reintroduction of price-wage controls.

Franklin Roosevelt's formation of a power base by combining farmer-labor support with quite a bit from industry left the government littered with an unprecedented multiplication of these clientele-oriented bureaus and agencies—each with Congressional supporters. It took some time for people to realize how frequently conflicting purposes were incorporated in two or more of these bureaus. In some degree this phenomenon has persisted, with vested interests extraordinarily difficult to unseat. Today the same cross-purposes appeared in the way the Democrats cultivated the blacks, and Nixon, the blue collar workers. These latter probably constituted the most implacable group opposed to forced busing in the interest of school integration.

In connection especially with Senate confirmation of appointments, "conflict of interest" has come to be a concept with a real cutting edge. Disclosures of investments and past connections of key appointees reach the level of the Cabinet and the White House staff at confirmation hearings.

"Creative conflict" is a working concept useful to Presidents, key administrators, and Congress in search of a "best" policy. There is general recognition today among administrators of competence that broadly based, goal-oriented departments are not only the best solution to counter the evils of bureau-clientele relationships; they may be the only practicable solution. An alternative is to build up the OMB and other relevant branches of the inner Presidency, and, if necessary, introduce a permanent evaluation and planning staff. The two solutions are not mutually exclusive. Even if such departments are created, there will still be interdepartmental problems.[2]

One other administrative area was suggested with possibilities for tempering or filtering out some of the shortcomings of our special interest pattern. This appeared occasionally in the discussion and in the literature dealing with organization and structure. This was the recent formation of Regional Councils with representatives of the various departments plus a White House representative to assure command and control.[3]

These assure more frequent meetings across departmental lines of those whose policies affect each other at the grass roots.

There is another aspect of pluralism which favors the continuance or establishment of discrete centers of power in the government. There is really a battle of the first magnitude at the present time looking, not to the widening of the scope of departments, but to their dismemberment.

There is pressure on HEW for its division into a Department or Agency of Social Security, and departments of Health and Education. Proposals to incorporate the Small Business Administration into the present weakened Department of Commerce are fought vigorously. Aviation protagonists want the Federal Aviation Administration detached from the Department of Transportation. We have already referred to the succcessful efforts of advocates of special attention to a given function in securing its inclusion in the Executive Office. What hornet's nests would be stirred up by a general program of goal-oriented, comprehensive departments can be imagined. Nixon's program was first treated as unbelievable, but bits and pieces of analysis and hearings were in progress when Watergate took over. In such consolidations, the contracting of a President's span of control always has its appeal in the White House, especially to the President and the OMB. Congress at least initially is more congenial to fragmentation. It fits better its organization by specialized committees and subcommittees, and leads it to think, perhaps correctly, that its rival policy leverage over against the Presidency gains thereby. Congress definitely wants certain kinds of purposes represented at high levels. Theirs are difficult arguments to combat, except by countering with a more impressive argument than "span of control." Only the overriding national interest, and perhaps the leverage it might give to goal-oriented party programs, would seem to carry enough real weight to disturb the existing arrangements by which senior Conressmen have apportioned power. If the splintering continues, the power to propose resolution of interagency conflicts will inevitably gravitate to the White House.

Much discussion at Airlie centered on the apparently unanimous belief that the President reflected the national mood and interest better than Congress. If perspectives are limited to great issues, there is little doubt as to its truth. On the other hand, there is much to be said for Congress in this connection. In the case of legislative proposals of relatively minor concern to the President, he may be expected to refer them to the bureaus most involved. Such a bureau almost inevitably will approach the question with certain predispositions. It may even have been the ultimate origin of the proposal. Because of specialization in Congress and the wide span of knowledge and experience represented in its members, there is the near-certainty that someone will turn up with a special angle on the problem. Because the Congressional staff resources are less likely to be biased, the combination of member and staff may well tilt the scales in a different direction. Even on major issues, the Congressional system is likely to turn up points which will improve a bill as it left the White House with recommendation for enactment. On the other hand, such amendments may be too special-interest-oriented, but not important enough to the members as a whole to receive thorough consideration. Congress viscerally does not like to hurt any group, however minor, that feels deeply about anything. It would rather omit or add a clause dealing with the objection and achieve a consensus.

Reform groups (usually elitist) and intellectuals (usually liberal) have been listened to as critics of the pluralistic influence in the subsystems and the government generally. They believe three things must be institutionalized by the Presidency to cope with the problem: an independent evaluating mechanism, an effective interdepartmental clearing and coordinating mechanism, and long-range planning. Departmental reorganizations along goal-oriented lines and regional councils in the field could well be added.

NOTES

1. For the "whirlpool" factor in generation of policy, See Ernest S. Griffith, *Impasse of Democracy* (New York, Harrison—Hilton 1939), p. 182ff.

2. See Chapter 16 for a fuller discussion and Chapter 17 for Nixon's proposals.

3. See Chapter 18 for a fuller discussion.

CHAPTER 15

Communications and Roadblocks

A problem that plagues all big and complex governments is the failure of communication. Why? A few generalizations contain the key to most of this. Bigness and complexity always present the problem of not enought time.
Key executives, from the President on down, are almost all
overcommitted. What suffers is that either last-minute or,
for that matter, "first-minute" decisions are apt to be pre-
empted by the seeming logic of the first person the executive consults. He may originally have intended to secure all
reasonable options, before committing himself. Yet his
desk piles up and his appointments calendar is filled. It
becomes easier to make a spot decision when first he is confronted by a problem and the adviser has an answer ready.
Nixon and Kissinger, as was brought out earlier, originally
had an excellent system of developing options and a Senior
Review Group to consider them. But time pressed more
and more; Kissinger had less and less time. He found himself bypassing the reviewing stage and either making the
decision himself, or suggesting one to the President minus
options, which no one had had the time to develop. Then,
too, Kissinger was more and more away from Washington,
and the established NSC processes tended more and more
to atrophy. Thus Nixon might himself make a decision virtually unaided, or on the sole recommendation of a staff

specialist. This attrition of the intent to have options developed was characteristic of executives all down the line. Time was the enemy. The one who had the first or the customary access to his chief was increasingly determinative.

Another characteristic block to adequate communication was deliberate preemption of access to the decision-maker on the part of a subject-matter specialist or even by his own "administrative assistant." Humility rarely characterizes either breed.

Departmental jealousy was another obstacle. A particular department may wish to preempt a domain which also concerns other agencies, and presents the latter with a *fait accompli*. There has been no one in a position to say, "Wait a minute. Shouldn't so-and-so be brought into the act?" A broadened participation in a decision becomes both a threat and a complication.

An executive may start out with the determination that certain persons should be seen regularly, and certain bodies or councils should meet regularly. This was one function of regular Cabinet meetings, and of the President meeting regularly with the party leadership of Congress. Again the full calendar of appointments, the urgent crisis, a pressing engagement, an out-of-town trip, or a distinguished guest—these and other matters caused postponements. From this arose irregularity in meetings. "Irregularity" became "infrequent," and these all-important lines of communication were often atrophied with quite serious consequences.

Classified material in foreign relations, a program crisis in domestic affairs, become excuses for not informing, or for lying to, the press and public. When this happens, confidence weakens.

Perhaps the executive is not really interested in *persons*, but only in objectives. The subtle rapport that arises in human terms when you believe the man who gives you a directive cares also about you, is lost—and communication of the spirit is missing.

Insecurity, a fear of being "handled," continual experience that one of your subordinates is always trying to sell
you a bill of goods—these impair communication.

The overconfidence that Nixon felt after his landslide
victory made him cut corners, short-circuit the contacts
necessary to establish real cooperation; and he lost
Congressional support. Lack of attention to communication was among the factors blocking what he hoped
would be a second-term program.

Numerous other places in which failures in communication have led to failures or shortfalls in accomplishment
have already been noted in the earlier chapters. A list
might be impressive, but the point is already clear. We turn
therefore to identifying the specific relationships where
communication is especially important. With the President
himself is a good place to start. William Carey pictured his
predicament in the following terms: "There he sits, over-
worked and making the best of a bad situation, while all
around him his princes and serfs are doing and undoing in
thousands of actions the work of his administration without his having a clue."[1] In other words, the failures were
the products of the absence of any effective system of
information. The Ash Commission had included such a
system in its recommendations.

Once again, we can picture the near-panacea that
seemed to present itself in the form of the Domestic
Council. No longer would the Cabinet complain of lack of
access, or that one of its members had stolen a march on
others in these latters' domain. There would be, as in the
NSC, staff to develop options. Communication in the
domestic field would be institutionalized, as it had allegedly
been in the NSC. Interdepartmental committees with staff
could communicate progress, recommendations, and
decisions to their chiefs.

Efforts at outreach to upper and middle management at
the regional level had had some success under Kennedy in
the formation of Federal Executive Boards in ten
metropolitan areas. Johnson let them wither. Nixon
revived the plan in somewhat different form. Each Region-

al Council so established was assigned a White House representative to help conformity to central directives.

A communications system might also help the President in explicit assignment of tasks in the inner Presidency. Perhaps Nixon felt that the tapes would provide an adequate record of his directives in this regard, and might take the place of the written record that Truman kept.

As regards the "inner Cabinet" and also with HEW, the communication was not too bad under Nixon. As for the others and agency heads (except Roy Ash), he used his surrogates to give orders and receive questions. Access to the President was basically denied them. Nixon feared that they would only ask something for their agency, and that the career service had seduced them in any event.

Such "exile" on this scale was new. Secretary Robert Weaver, for example, told how he never had any difficulty in seeing both Kennedy and Johnson whenever he asked. He said that he did try to hold down his requests to the really important matters. Why Cabinet members under Nixon did not resign in protest may have been an indication that this outer Cabinet was not one of strong men. The specialists on the White House staff were actively dealing with the staffs of the Cabinet and sub-Cabinet in situations in which the President had little interest. Predictably this made these White House men cordially disliked in certain quarters.

Communication between Nixon and the Congress also deteriorated steadily, even with its leaders. He or his staff escalated the extent of classified material, often to the detriment of his program. The reasonably satisfactory relationships—approximated by most of his predecessors—have already been outlined.[2] Historically these relationships were somewhat favored at the times at which both branches were of the same party—but this has been less of a factor in recent years.

The problems of communication between the political appointees at the upper level of the departments and agencies and their senior career service have already been noted, and the ideal relationships pointed out. One might

at this point add another hazard, probably never sur-
mounted completely in any administration. Because of
mutual suspicion it probably reached its nadir under
Nixon. This is presented by the interposition of staff "layering" between the President and the department heads. It
is difficult enough to establish communication and
rapport down long hierarchical lines in any event. Something is almost bound to be lost in transit. There is a better
chance if the agency head really has a first hand share in
his President's developing program. Clarity and certainty
become assets which can be communicated.

There may be something to be said at this point for the
two-hat man, who is both counselor to the President and
head of an agency. He will obviously need two desks as well
as two hats to be effective. An agency head also needs a
first-class Under Secretary—perhaps two, one for policy
and one for administration. The latter will surely, if he
knows his responsibilities, see that the agency has a functioning communications system.

One of the most interesting and valuable recent usages
in the government (not discussed at Airlie for lack of time)
is the communications system set up for transition and
continuity between outgoing and incoming administrations. Hoover offered such cooperation to Roosevelt, but
the latter refused. The system began when Eisenhower
accepted a similar offer from Truman, and has continued
since them. It is probably now well established.

Actually the idea is very simple. The incoming President
is invited to designate such persons as he may wish, to
observe the workings of each major unit, to learn of its
problems, and quite possibly to share in some of the
decisions. Ideally those chosen should be among those who
will have at least a share of the responsibility for the function under the new administration. Transitions have been
much more smoothly consummated since this practice was
introduced.

Finally, it may be of use to identify the most usual
sources of bias in communications. It is obviously of great

importance to the President and to all those associated directly or indirectly with the Institutional Presidency that they be aware of those relationships most likely to be subject to such bias.

Perhaps the chief source of bias is loyalty to one's agency and program, including serving its clientele. This may be quite unconscious, but those with whom spokesmen of an agency deal must be aware of the danger. Nixon, in fact, may have overreacted in this regard.

A second source has already been mentioned—the fear on the part of subordinate staff to "tell it like it is" to their chief, if he doesn't want even to hear a point of view that does not coincide with his own. He may well have been known to penalize those differing with him.

A third source is a hasty, premature commitment to a point of view, concerning which the person in question thereafter feels defensive about challenges.

All of the foregoing often infect even the research process and foreordain the conclusions.

Some points of view seem to their holders to be so kept from a President that they feel it necessary to demonstrate—or even riot—to bring them to his attention.

To those already in favored positions with a President, independent advisers constitute a threat. If they have their way, these "interlopers" will probably be downgraded or banned altogether. The selection and composition of task forces are important in this connection. Are they to be a cross-section of the qualified and concerned, or are they to be "packed" to assure the kind of result a President or his surrogate wishes?

Lack of time is usually chiefly reponsible for Executive reliance on biased advice. The remedy is fairly simple and has already been mentioned in other connections. It is for the Executive to insist on being presented with honest options at the time of decision. If it is practicable, he might well structure an adversary relationship, with the protagonists fighting it out in his presence. Conflict is an important means of communication.

As regards the education of the general public, such conflict is far more likely to emerge from Congress in its debates and hearings than from an Executive Branch. The latter is ostensibly dedicated to presenting a monolithic image to the public. Incidentally, this offers a constant challenge to the news media to ferret out the internal quarrels within the Executive. Hence the calculated leak, usually from those who are losing the internal battle.

In thinking through the content of this particular chapter, the author wonders whether it should have been a separate chapter in the first place. Much of what has been said here has also been included elsewhere, incidental to other topics. The fact is that the problem of communications is present all through the Institutional Presidency. It is a dimension of success or failure in all the major inter-relationships. But this constant recurrence of types of success or types of failure itself justifies their sharpened identification.

NOTES

1. William D. Carey, "Presidential Staffing in the Sixties and Seventies," *Public Administration Review* (1969), p. 452.

2. See Chapter 9. For communications (and lack of it) with the media, see Chapter 12.

Chapter 16

The Problems of New and Interdepartmental Functions

"No one principle ever exhausts the meaning of a complex situation."[1] This is the cardinal sin in simplistic ethics; it is the major premise of situational ethics.

So also no single government agency—existing or projected—ever (or hardly ever) is comprehensive enough in its own right to handle a complex problem—unless in some fashion or other it can call upon the insights and count upon the aid of related agencies. This is the nature of today's world.

Can agencies—especially goal-related agencies—be developed adequately, on their own to devise and carry out a program to reach a goal?

On a macro scale, even a goal so comprehensive as the increase in our GNP (gross national product) fails to take into account the three interrelated goals of an equitable distribution of the product, the quality of life, and the needs of future generations. In other words, it provides no guarantee of justice and foresight.

There is also the pervading, endemic dichotomy[2] between the goals, aspiration, and values of the departments and those of the White House. In resolving this dichotomy, the operating experience and technical competence of the departments are certainly needed. The final decisions ought to be made at the White House level. Its planning and program have a better chance to take a more comprehensive and longer-range view. Insofar as Congress rightly claims a share in these decisions, it is caught in its own schizophrenic dilemma of its "filter function" and its rash of subsystems.

The Institutional Presidency is riddled with these problems. They arise in an especially acute form whenever the decision to add a new function is made. During 1965–66 there was an extraordinary outpouring of legislation which entangled every department. Categorical grants proliferated; overlapping jurisdictions were everywhere. The Heineman Task Force put its finger on the problem in the postaudit of these, the Great Society programs of President Johnson. So much had been hoped from them; and the hopes of so many were disappointed. Their diagnosis is well worth summarizing:

1. The principal target problems were poverty, discrimination against minorities and the powerless, urban blight, pollution of air and water. These were not, and could not be, the sole concern of any one department. Nor would any of them yield even to a series of isolated program efforts from many departments.

2. The Federal social programs remain badly coordinated in both Washington and the field. There are wars as to jurisdiction, and related programs in target areas that fail to mesh at all.

3. The social problems are in the field, but the administrations are concentrated in Washington. These administrations are in autonomous bureaus below the Presidential and departmental level.

Recommendations followed from the diagnosis, and will be fused with those from other sources.[3]

There were other reasons for the failure of the programs. There was a lack of knowledge, even by the experts, in certain fields. Improving education in the ghetto will serve as an example. Little or no progress was registered in spite of the multiplicity of programs and the large expenditures. Then, too, our nation is too large and too diverse for uniform answers to its local problems.

Universal rules may well do more harm than good. Johnson as well as Nixon became so preoccupied with foreign affairs that neither gave adequate attention to the domestic. Neither really saw through their programs. Nixon felt many of Johnson's were so hopelessly clogged or demonstrably failing that he proceeded to dismantle them. Califano did his best as surrogate for Johnson. Ehrlichman was his lineal successor for Nixon.

With this background, what are the problems facing a President whenever a new program is proposed? Assume he finds it attractive. He has decided in his own mind to go ahead with it. One of the first questions is whether to establish a new agency or to give it to one of the existing departments. Assuming he decides on the first alternative, shall it be in the Executive Office for the time being or independent? If he opts for the second alternative, which department? In each of these decisions we assume (a doubtful assumption) that he will have taken extended counsel in the course of which options will have been developed.

In the process, certain political factors will have entered in. Which alternative will be most likely to commend itself to Congress? Shall its administration, with great leeway for decisions, be devolved to state and local governments, leaving the federal government largely concerned with grants-in-aid, and their terms—detailed or general? If the proposal has originally emanated from an existing department or agency, shall "adversaries" from other departments, his own staff, or outsiders be called in? These would present possible options to the original recommendations—especially as to location of responsibility. Should he refer it to the OMB or the Domestic Council for further research? If the latter, should it set up an interdepartmental committee with staff to study these questions of location, function, and procedures for continual interrelations and cooperation? Do the uncertainties call for a "pilot project" before final judgment?

In adoptions of a new program, certain common
elements are usually present. One is the interagency
struggle for power. Does vocational education belong in
the Department of Labor or the Office of Education?
Who shall enforce civil rights and in what fashion? Shall
the distribution of surplus food be used primarily to help
agriculture price stability or for short-term foreign policy
goals (Agriculture vs. State or Defense)? Who shall
determine the guidelines for the "model cities" program,
when several categories and several departments are
involved—or shall they be freely delegated to the cities
themselves under special revenue sharing? The whole
model cities program at its launching furnished classic
examples of "how not to do it." HEW had a major role in
its execution and was to furnish 30 to 50 percent of its
funding. They were not brought into the development
process, and later even their budget officer was excluded.
Shall a tariff be raised or lowered? Bundy called the
Executive Branch more nearly "a collection of badly
separated principalities, than a single instrument of
executive action." We must bear this characterization in
mind, not only in connection with new programs, but even
more in proposals for restructuring the whole Institutional Presidency.

Once a decision has been made, account must always be
taken that sabotage may be lurking in the wings from
those not called on stage.

The career service is probably better in locating these
problems than are the political chiefs. How to stimulate
their reporting through channels (or by bypassing the
channels) is a problem in itself.

All recent Presidents have frequently opted for a new
agency in the beginning. It has many apparent advantages. The urgency factor is often present, notably in wartime. We have recently witnessed a whole series of energy-
related agencies; and these at first were located in the
Executive Office to emphasize their importance and to
assure Presidential attention. It is always attractive to

appoint a "czar," and in wartime this often worked. For example, note the effective work done in the "War on rubber."

One "advantage" is that civil service procedures can be bypassed, as delaying a new agency's functioning. The extent to which this is a disadvantage depends upon the subsequent administration of the agency's personnel policy. The Civil Service Commission can give very considerable help outside its normal procedures, if the new agency wishes it.

Quite possibly the agency initially should in fact be outside an existing department in order to give it a flexibility apart from habitual bureaucratic behavior. There will be time enough later to assign it to a department, when it becomes apparent with which it is most appropriately linked. Meanwhile an interagency coordinating committee can be set up chaired by a neutral or an appropriate agency's head. This should report to the White House. There is an area of uncertainty at this point about to precisely whom the new agency should report, or who in the White House should monitor the committee to make certain communication and cooperation are in fact proceeding. Alternatives are the OMB, the Domestic Council, or a Presidential assistant specifically assigned. Unless the interdepartmental committee can agree, jurisdictional disputes will normally reach the White House. It may be found that the disputes are in fact intradepartmental, or obviously belong to the NSC to resolve. In any event the center to resolve the dispute may need staff, some of whom are furnished from a neutral source.

The case for assignment of the new function to an existing department is obvious, from the standpoint of economy and (hopefully) lessening jurisdictional disputes. This latter is by no means asssured. If Congress by way of its Public Works or Interior and Insular Affairs committees assigns new functions in water resources to the Army Engineers or the Bureau of Reclamation, one can usually count on the Agriculture Committees advocating rival powers for the Soils Conservation Service. Many beneficiaries of the implicit federal subsidies like it this way—for the rival agencies may bid higher and higher grants or expenditures so as to be the chosen instrument in a given project.

There have been many ways in the past to handle interagency relationships. There still are. It is profitable to pass these options in review.

Probably the earliest was the interagency committee. This was usually established by executive order, if at least semipermanent, or occasionally by statute. There were at one time (and probably still are) between 1,000 and 2,000 such committees on the books. For a while the Legislative Reference division of the old Bureau of the Budget served as a kind of switch board to spot areas of potential interagency overlap or conflicting purposes. As new agencies multiplied, it lost control. Its staff was too small for the functional explosions of recent years. OMB is attempting to recapture this monitoring or coordinating function. The Domestic Council is a probable rival.

One of the crying needs of these interdepartmental committees has been staff services, especially during the early years in which patterns of coordination must be established. Without such staff or an overriding authority, each agency tended covertly or openly to rationalize its own duplicating sector, and in any event to be reluctant to cooperate with its perceived rivals.

An early attempt to put teeth into such an interagency committee was to designate a "lead agency" for all such interagency committees. It did not work in foreign policy, for example, for State, as has been remarked earlier,[4] was not equipped staff-wise or temperamentally to assume such responsibility. In the first two or three years of the Nixon-Kissinger national security partnership, lines of responsibility, staff assignments, deadlines, and directives were very clear for the many interdepartmental committees set up to develop options. At a later stage, Kissinger himself chaired the important review and policy bodies—except the NSC itself, which the President headed.

Much of the strength of these NSC committees lay in their staffs. This would point in the direction of the Domestic Council as the logical parent for policy forming interdepartmental committees in its field. It would need a considerably larger staff pool than it now has, and one the members of which had the competences for the purpose. Some examples of interagency problems already finding their way to the DC were on the subjects of drugs, welfare reform (involving HEW, Labor, etc.) in which options were (or are to be) developed, early work in the energy area, and the economy.

Some committees have been transferred to the field level (in the same town), and some policy control added in the person of a chairman. It was hoped also that this might lessen the pressures leading to the Congressional-clientele-bureaucracy subsystems.

There are really only two effective options, although variants exist in both. These are arbitration or control in the White House or Executive Office, or departmental reorganization into superdepartments patterned after Defense. They are not mutually exclusive, for no department could possibly be comprehensive enough to embrace all the potential points of overlap or cooperation. There must still be a role for the inner Presidency.

The conferees at Airlie were in mild disagreement as to the form this control should take. One suggestion was that there be a minimum of two of the Bundy-Sorensen type—one for international and one for domestic affairs—on the President's own staff. They would deal with interdepartmental affairs and assist the President in making policy and seeing to it that this policy was carried out. They could work with the NSC and the DC respectively. The one who made the suggestion was the first to admit that the lines between the two fields were increasingly blurred. There was also criticism that no one person could be found in the domestic field with skills comparable to

Bundy or Kissinger. This presently held true of both the
OMB and the DC. The function of guiding a committee in
its development of options would clearly need more than
one person, and they must be of a special type. They must
have a capacity to think *institutionally*, as well as having
some subject-matter expertise. Typical skills were those of
a budget officer, an economic adviser, a student of the
impact of science. The President's own staff must not be
larger than he can personally deal with. (There was dis-
sent expressed with this limitation, but the distinction in
type was not opposed.) There was general agreement that
the function of planning in advance should be available
somewhere—either *ad hoc* (perhaps by a task force) or by a
permanent unit in the Executive Office. Thus interagency
problems, by being identified in advance in many
instances, would be considerably lessened in frequency
and degree of friction. Inconsistencies could be identified
and avoided. Responsibility could be clearly assigned for
carrying out the plan.

As matters had stood in the Nixon administration, the
White House staff had been too large, and at the same
time, quite deficient in effective troubleshooters. The
result had been too much meddling in interagency problems. Another seriously complicating factor was that the
problems were more and more settled at the White House
level without even bringing the concerned agency heads
into the picture.

Some transfers of bureaus from one agency to another
might aid in a solution. The famous borderline example
has been the Forest Service. It has shuttled between Agriculture and Interior; and if the latter is renamed the
Department of Energy and Natural Resources, it may
shuttle again.

The "superdepartment" has already been discussed
elsewhere.[5] It will appear again as one of the major
reforms proposed by Nixon. For the time being, its Nixon
sponsorship has secured its tabling. Such a solution would
be excellent from the standpoint of settling many inter-

agency disputes at a lower level, so that the White House is not clogged with them. However, it faces formidable opponents in Congress. Several committee chairmen "ganged up" against a Department of Community Development. The proposal for a Department of Energy and Natural Resources carried too much "baggage." HEW and Defense are such comprehensive departments already, and do function in the fashion described. All recent studies have come out for such major-purpose departments. The phrase "goal-oriented" is used interchangeably. Such a solution delegates arbitration, but does not necessarily eliminate the subsystems. These latter may— as in HEW—merely bide their time to tear such a department apart.

Councils in the Executive Office—and the NSC and the DC—have the advantage of already existing as actual and potential sources of analysis of interagency problems. This they have done by committees set up under their sponsorship and with staff furnished. The DC's future is fragile. It has been predicted that it would take many years to realize its potential.

There are other possible options that have been mentioned in dealing with these interagency problems. An Assistant President (for Administration) has support in some knowledgeable quarters. It also has been denounced as contrary to the American system. The rehabilitation of the Legislative Reference unit in OMB, with a more adequate management staff and perhaps renamed, is OMB's alternative to the DC. It does not bring in the department heads. The Cabinet secretariat might be revived, enlarged, and assigned such a function, but the Cabinet is itself moribund. A Federal Executive Service, with its presumed rotation of personnel among the agencies, could ease problems on an *ad hoc* basis. Such rotation might well contribute in any event to better relations between the departments. The United Nations Association came out in favor of the two-hats solution of Kissinger. How far it might be applicable to other departments, and bring together their secretaries more frequently and intimately (either as White House Counselors or Assistants or informally) is at present a "far out" possibility. Most of the Airlie conferees were in favor of dropping the two-hats already worn!

Eisenhower simply abolished the National Aeronautics and Space Council. But Johnson brought it back.

There are those who in certain situations would retain duplication so as to promote rivalry as assuring better results. The intelligence field and water resource management have been mentioned in this connection.

Those writing and thinking concerning interagency problems have with rare exceptions been biased in favor of the Executive Branch viewpoint. Probably a majority of this majority favor national solutions over a delegation of ultimate decisions to the states and localities. There is, however, considerable sentiment for reducing greatly the numbers of grants by category, through grouping or combining many of them. This, in itself, would seem to give the lesser units more leeway, but the real question is how far central control would still be retained.

Congress has few defenders as regards this interrelated functional aspect of governance. "Congress is not amenable to ordering" is a characteristic statement: one, incidentally, which might be challenged; but there are other values besides logical order which ought also to be taken into account, if the introductory paragraphs of this chapter are valid. Local adaptations, clienteles otherwise unrepresented, experimental ventures, all may lurk in the subsystems, as well as their less happy by-products—and then again, they may not!

NOTES

1. The late Isaiah Bowman, then president of John Hopkins University.
2. See Chapter 14.
3. See p. 234.
4. See p. 69.
5. See pp. 155–156.

Chapter 17

Some Recent Problems:
Trends or Pathology?
(Secrecy, Intelligence, Malfeasance,
Political Activities)

A whole cluster of problems recently and suddenly took on the cumulative aspect of a national crisis. The system of government, the meaning of public interest, a lack of basic integrity in and around the President, have called into question the Institutional Presidency itself. Has this reaction over-reached itself? Should we speak of what has come to be known as "Watergate" as a historical trend or an abnormal situation belonging in the realm of pathology?

Arthur M. Schlesinger, Jr.'s book *The Imperial Presidency* has called the Nixon Presidency "not an aberration but a culmination." This has influenced many people to opt for the "trend" theory and to ask what to do now.

"Dirty tricks" in campaigns were not only not unknown. They were common in our state and local political campaigns of the latter decades of the last century. They have persisted to the present day at least as an occasional phenomenon. The defeat of Senator Joseph Tydings of Maryland by a fake photograph was notorious less than twenty years ago. Nixon himself called off the investigation of alleged voting frauds in the 1960 Presidential campaign involving the electoral votes of Texas and Illinois—quite possibly enough to have elected him instead of Kennedy.

Perhaps the most extreme general claim of "executive privilege" was made by President Eisenhower, but he did

not act upon it. Other Presidents, before Nixon, had
vested surrogate powers in their staff. Other Presidents
had claimed an undefined residual power under the
Constitution in the national interest in an emergency, but
had sought subsequent Congressional approval. The
courts had restrained President Truman from seizure of
the steel plants.

What then was the difference? It was a succession or
accumulation of actions, some of which had in fact
occurred in other administrations. Most striking were the
eventual proof of Nixon's continual lying to the American
people to cover up his participation in an illegal cover-up,
dubious income tax returns[1] , illegal activites by his campaign committee, waffling for a while as to whether he
would accept a Supreme Court decision short of unanimity, denial of the tapes which contained the key to his
own guilt as well as that of his associates, unauthorized
break-ins and wiretaps, the loss of his cases on repeated
major "impoundment" of appropriations, approval (at
least for a short time) of use of an "enemies" list for selective audit of income tax returns and other harassment. But
why continue the catalogue? Nixon resigned under fire,
but still without admitting legal or moral guilt. His successor pardoned him in advance for all offenses which might
subsequently be exposed.

Quite possibly there was a pathological element involved
for which there was no real precedent. Out of a fear of the
rioting and demonstrations, egged on apparently by some
of his White House staff, the President developed a kind of
siege mentality. Assuming he had had no advance notice of
the Watergate episode itself, he was faced with a choice
involving a clear judicial process dangerous to his closest
and most loyal associates, those upon whom he had
learned to depend for so many things. There was also the
possibility that disclosure at the time might threaten his
own re-election. The tapes thus far have not revealed any
evidence that he felt deeply that the welfare of the country
might be involved in such re-election. This was apparently

not an overriding factor, but seems not to have been a factor at all in the attempted cover-up. Nor did the tapes seem ever to have mentioned either ethical considerations or the public interest. Moreover his massive concern over leaks, his insatiable appetite for political intelligence, and the "do it yourself" attitude regardless of law had an ambience with pathological overtones.

Suspicion and resentment at some of the bureaucracy's resistance to the executive program were quite usual with recent Presidents. Impoundments were specifically upheld in a House resolution in the 1940s—but never on the scale used by Nixon. Even on this scale, he would probably have been upheld in Congress on the economy issue had he not offended in so many other ways. The intended use of the budget to wipe out the specifically authorized Office of Economic Opportunity was new. But pressure from Congress resulted in its retention as an entity for the time being.

There was no question that there was a crisis. There is unfortunately also no question that the immediacy of the crisis has now passed, because our system of government held together and its checks and balances worked. Some would say it worked too slowly. Others would say that only a series of fortunate events saved it—the finding of the bugged room, the assignment of Judge John Sirica to the case, the preservation and locating of the tapes, the persistance of the special prosecutors. But the correctives contemplated in the system did work.

The courts did their part. The Supreme Court including Nixon's own appointees upheld the demands for relevant tapes. The House proceeded in thorough, orderly fashion to set the impeachment process in motion. There was a full sense of its responsibility on the part of the impeachment subcommittee. The President resigned. The device of a special prosecutor eventually immune from removal was hit upon to assure that the judicial process would not be impaired by anyone who might feel himself under any obligation to Nixon. A new Vice-President was found and confirmed, when the first one resigned in a forced plea-bargaining. Congress (specifically the Senate through the Ervin Committee) conducted its own exhaustive inquiry on illegal and unwholesome election practics. This resulted in a number of indictments and convictions, and in a far-reaching new Campaign Reform Act. A solution to the impoundment problem was incorporated in the Congressional Budget and Impoundment Control Act. Safeguards against use of troops in combat without Congressional authorization were included in the War Powers Act. This act was primarily motivated by Vietnam, and traced itself to President Johnson and the Gulf of Tonkin resolution. It is too early to say whether it will serve its purpose. Class action suits are proving an effective weapon to induce the Executive Branch to obey the law.

In any event, the Legislative and Judicial branches functioned according to the Constitution, and new metes and bounds have been set to Presidential powers. It will be some time before a President is likely to test their outer limits again in defiance of Congress. Nixon himself finally accepted the historic role of the Supreme Court as denying his own interpretation of a Presidential prerogative of unlimited executive privilege. This included the claimed power to determine which records (including tapes) must be yielded to Congress or the courts.

But many of the recent events still have no clear and final boundaries set—and may never have. These include classification of information, leaks, limits and control of intelligence activities, executive privilege, government malfeasance in politicizing the judicial process, unacceptable campaign activites. They remain in the area of potentially serious, but discussable problems.

Secrecy—that is, the classification of information with varying limitations as to its availability—is a recognized practice in all governments. The British, for example, under their Official Secrets Act probably use it much more extensively as regards intragovernmental communications than do we. "Any information which you come in command of as a result of your official position you cannot give to an unauthorized person." While Eisenhower claimed an unlimited right to extend executive privilege to any and all such material, he was normally completely cooperative in releasing material which Congress felt was useful or necessary for legislative purposes. He did oppose Congressional committee oversight of the CIA.

No one seems to oppose in principle such classification in time of war, if in any way the release of material would aid the enemy. Sometimes our government has found it to its advantage to "leak" false material even to Congress to fool the enemy. This was done in the case of the invasion of Sicily. Concealment or false information to maintain morale on the home front raises other questions. President Johnson is alleged to have kept back much information concerning Vietnam, because in his judgment it would have impaired public and Congressional support of the war. Most people would probably fault him for this in retrospect.

Defense and State and, of course, the CIA classify much of their information—some of it "wholesale" and automatically, although State releases much of this (also automatically) after a set period of years. Defense would probably not find this practicable. The FBI classifies almost all of its records on persons, because so much of it consists of unauthenticated rumors. In all probability, most agencies proceed on the basis "When in doubt, classify," although directives have been issued in the Department of Defense for the opposite approach.

There are two major problems in this connection. The first involves Defense. To declassify the mass of existing classified material is really an inordinately expensive process. Probably as regards most of this material, nobody really would care to use it, as it is out of date. The second problem involves all agencies. Congress has attempted through legislation to unstop any roadblock to access to material which it might want to use in an investigation, or which would be in the public interest to make generally available. Agency reluctance usually stems from one of two reasons, neither of which Congress finds very impressive. One of these is when an agency wants to cover up a mistake. The other involves material which its clientele or a pressure group might find compromising. A special case arises when an agency is interested in research material in a given field, and obtains it from specific individuals or corporations on the promise that the summary of the information from all sources will not disclose (for example) "trade secrets" of a particular corporation or the identity of the individuals responding. Special regulations govern the availability of individual and corporate income tax returns, and of personnel office records.

It was alleged that the branches of the armed services leak material detrimental to their rivals.

There is wide difference of opinion as to whether an individual in possession of classified material should ever leak it to the press or Congress, and whether the former, knowing it to be a "leak," should publish it. At the Airlie conference, the range was from a full penalty for the leaker (including the press), to a kind of selective waffle, "if the public interest were served thereby." No one could really define this, although some conferees defended the leak of the Pentagon Papers on this ground. The hardest question to answer was when a leak is a matter of conscience; but no one responded to a statement that under these circumstances the person must be prepared to take the consequences. Whenever the question was raised otherwise, it was answered by generalizations that were not self-defining. Most people took refuge in a statement that too much was classified and more declassification was desirable. One participant said he would encourage leaks, but another answered that the more leaks you have, the more rigid limits would be put on the number of people allowed access in line of duty. This would defeat the purpose of communication, in cases in which it was most needed.

When the *Chicago Tribune* leaked the Japanese purple

code, they would have been indicted, had the Japanese noticed it. *The Times-Herald* was about to be indicted for printing Senator Burton Wheeler's leak to them of our war plans; but Pearl Harbor came along, and they were saved. The press has simply refused to grapple with the problem of categorizing what leaks they believe they would be justified and what unjustified in printing. So the problem remains virtually insurmountable.

Another question discussed in this connection was the extent to which Congress could be trusted. The administration has always been opposed to a Congressional committee overseeing intelligence. Until recently the Congressional leadership has agreed with the administration (except for Senator Mike Mansfield). However, the Armed Services and Foreign Relations committees for the most part have wished such a committee. Allen Dulles, the Director of the CIA, changed his mind, but could not convince Eisenhower.

If the Congressional committee charged with oversight is a large one, leaks are almost inevitable. There seems, however, to have been none from the Joint Committee on Atomic Energy, or from the Special (Nedzi) Subcommittee on Intelligence in the House and the (Stennis) Subcommittee on Central Intelligence in the Senate, whose province it was to oversee the CIA. Both the Nedzi and the Stennis committees did a conscientious job, but how far they probed or wished to probe into the details of "black activities" was not known. The statements were made that if it is really concerned, not only should classified information be available to an appropriate Congressional unit, but in fact almost all of it was. The member or members of the two appropriations committees who were informed of the Manhattan Project not only kept the secret, but also steered their colleagues away from indiscreet inquiries.

However, recent developments and disclosures, most of which emanated from the Senate committee headed by Senator Church, have not only downgraded past intelligence activities, but also cast doubt upon Congressional direction.

There also appears to be (or to have been) a joint informal committee of eight, two from each of the armed services committees and appropriations committees, also active in monitoring "black" activities. If such a permanent oversight committee were to be set up with the maximum safeguards, it should probably be constituted as a joint, bipartisan committee, with one or at the most two representatives from each of the Armed Services and the Foreign Relations and International Relations committees. They might be chosen jointly by the chairmen of the committees and the party leaderships. There would be a sufficient sense of responsibility in this group of selectors to assure that only those who could be trusted would be appointed. The adversary relationship is needed somewhere, and this would be as likely as anything to prevent activities such as the attempt to bribe the Chilean legislature. This latter has really done the United States great harm. The ultimate leak in this instance was Congressional. Apparently this had been approved by the committee chaired by Kissinger—unless this committee had been bypassed or the full nature of the proposed activity not disclosed. For some time, Presidents themselves have not been kept fully informed; but they may not have wished such full information, being ready to delegate the responsibility to those whom they trusted.

In the recent Foreign Assistance Act, it was provided that no funds should be available for covert activities, except as the President reports them to the International Relations and Foreign Relations committees.

There was some sentiment at Airlie that we should withdraw altogether from "black activities" and our intelligence agencies should confine themselves to estimates. This would probably be a popular move with the intellectual community. However, we know that our potential enemies are doing these things all the time. Perhaps we might confine our efforts to exposing *them*, but this might interfere with moves toward detente! Here is an excellent example of where simplistic answers simply will not do.

In any event the interest and concern of Congress are evident, as the presence of activity on the part of a half-dozen committees or subcommittees with responsibility in this area would indicate. There was the same ambivalence at Airlie regarding sanctions to prevent leaks. Sometimes it seems as though the discussion of questions of this character, like those of the leaks themselves, really mean that one approves of the leaks that one personally approves of in retrospect and is therefore against sanctions against their disclosure, and one disapproves of the leaks that one personally disapproves of in retrospect with the corollary attitude toward sanctions. The question is analogous to the one as to whether we should allow draft exemption for conscientious objectors to a *particular* war.

There are certain other questions involving the intelligence agencies, such as how many and where. How far does such duplication fall under the heading of the desirability of having options disclosed by the device of conflicting estimates? Such check and countercheck are important in this area, although the supervising committee or agency in the Executive (such as the NSC) could specify that the single agency must always include minority interpretations, if any, in its estimates.

The legal role of the FBI is in domestic affairs; of the CIA, foreign, including suspected foreign agents in the United States. An allegation did surface during the Watergate era that the President tried to mix the two in the cover-up. At time of writing, this aspect had not been thoroughly clarified. The law establishing each is clear as to the line of division, but its application is not. More recently serious charges have been made (and denied) that the CIA has extensive files on many American citizens who have participated in "radical" causes and riots.

The IRS records are available and usable under court order in criminal cases. To utilize IRS audits (other than for normal checks) as a method to harass an administration's opponents is inexcusable. Apparently Shultz as Secretary of the Treasury and the senior career service refused to be a party to this, and ignored the White House memoranda or requests in this area. There remains an unresolved problem as to the definition of "substantial" in the matter of tax exemption for nonprofit charitable, education, or public-service-oriented organizaions. If a "substantial" portion of their funds and effort is directed toward influencing legislation, they are ineligible. This does allow a subjective interpretation, in the event that someone in the Executive Branch (within or outside the IRS) disapproves of such an organization's principal purpose. The courts have not yet ruled, except in particular cases.

Executive privilege normally involves a dispute between Congress and the President. By Nixon's final acceptance of judicial supremacy as between the President and the judicial system, we may rather confidently regard any future disputes in this relationship as having been settled in favor of the judiciary. It is quite otherwise as regards availability of material to Congress, though the latter presumably has the option of throwing a particular case into the courts. It could do this by exercising its independent right to subpoena and, if necessary, arrest the Attorney General, who would then be released by a writ of habeas corpus under a court order. By appealing the order, a determination as to whether executive privilege applied in the particular case could be obtained from the court. Neither the President nor Congress has to date wished to press the matter to this extreme, one or the other preferring rather to waive its presumed rights in the interest of comity.

The desirability of a President insisting upon executive privilege would appear justified as regards interoffice memoranda or taped advice during the process of an executive from the President down making up his mind. Otherwise, such communications run the risk of either being destroyed, incomplete, uncandid, or otherwise distorted to the point of limiting their value. It might reach the extremes of either continual witch hunts, or a very serious impairment of the soundness of decisions. The extreme position that a President may unilaterally claim all executive business subject to his sole discretion as to when to invoke executive privilege can almost certainly not be sustained judicially. In any event it ought not to be used to cover up errors. Perhaps arbitration by the GAO as to whether the withholding did or did not come under this latter category might be accepted as reasonable by both sides, and as simpler than judicial procedure.

Legal delegation of Presidential authority has been held to be confined to those for whom confirmation by the Senate is required or who are supervised by such persons. On this basis a President who unilaterally gives powers of administration to his aides cannot then disavow their acts. There is a temptation to stretch executive privilege to cover this.

The courts have held that Congressional probings involving individuals, thereby threatening their civil rights, must have a legislative purpose. This sustains a category of use of executive privilege.

There are a number of serious questions involved when those in the government, especially the higher-ups, themselves break the law. Can the Department of Justice be trusted to prosecute? At present the answer is no.

Fortunately Watergate has produced what appears to be an adequate remedy for this—the special prosecutor. Obviously he must be protected by certain safeguards: confirmation by the Senate, tenure "for the duration of the crisis," legislative authorization for unlimited access to relevant material (this could be sustained by the courts, if challenged). There is a minority opinion favoring permanence (or a very long period) of tenure, for a special prosecutor with the post itself having a mandatory statutory base. However, probably an *ad hoc* mandate would be adequate, although the provision for *ad hoc* filling of such a post could be exempt from Presidential veto if permanent legislation (presumably signed by a President, or passed over his veto) authorized such an appointment whenever Congress by joint resolution shall determine. This eventuality would presumably arise after a Congressional committee, having conducted such investigation as lies within its power and competence, shall convince both houses of Congress of its necessity.

A new breed of public-interest lobbies and lawyers has arisen. These are likely to serve as adequate watchdogs of executive refusals to enforce certain laws or of selective enforcement influenced by partisan or other considerations. An example of such successful intervention has been the forcing of federal agencies to comply with various environmental protection laws requiring thorough "impact statements" prior to permitting certain constructions. These have included the Alaska pipeline, types of offshore drilling, nuclear power plants, nuclear testing for peaceful purposes, and a number of other challenged activities and permits. The illegality in question was not in the decisions, but in the fact that the decisions were made without impact statements. These statements had been required by law so as to allow public discussion and possible reconsideration—either as violating other provisions of environmental legislation, or inadvisable in any event on environmental grounds.

The use of wiretaps without court orders is now illegal in domestic affairs, even if the President orders them. We may reasonably expect such illegal use to cease in the future. Breaking into the office of Ellsberg's psychiatrist was also *ultra vires*. Executive interference in the process of justice resulted in the dismissal of the case against Ellsberg himself (otherwise quite possibly sound) for leaking the classified Pentagon Papers. Popkin, who participated, had no such ameliorating counterconsideration. A suit against the *New York Times* to enjoin against further publication of classified information was lost in the Supreme Court, on inconclusive and divided grounds. It left an opening for future prosecution for leaks with unpredictable results.

The career employees were virtually untarnished by the Watergate scandals. There is some evidence from both the FBI and IRS that career employees may have in fact circumscribed questionable activities advocated by their political superiors. The assumption that such restraint may be reasonably counted upon to be constant seems to be warranted. There have been occasional instances over the years where bribery of a career man has been proved, but they have been so rare as to warrant great confidence in the integrity of the permanent officials in our national government. This is quite a different matter from frequent conflicts in bureaucratic loyalty as between the President and Congress. This conflict of loyalty was at the root of Nixon's determination to make the White House the operational headquarters of the Executive Branch—the representative of *all* the people, as distinct from what he felt were the parochial interests of Congressmen and clientele-oriented bureaucrats.

There is another field which is to some extent a twilight zone. This is the utilization of the instrumentalities of the Executive Branch for partisan political purposes during a campaign. It has always been done by all recent Presidents and their politically appointed associates, with various self-imposed limits. The formal drawing up of lists of potential activities within various agencies, which would have a favorable reaction in the next campaign, may have been new in its formality; it was certainly not new in most of its suggestions. Assistance to Congressional candidates in marginal districts, not only by speeches in their favor, but by administrative decisions favorable to their districts prior to election day, has been universally practiced in recent years. So has the timing of more comprehensive decisions favorable to certain groups. Such was the announcement of an increase in the support price of milk to win the support of—and presumably illegal campaign contributions from—the organized dairy farmers. The blatant nature of the bargain will probably result in indictments.

The illegal nature of corporate campaign contributions

seems to have directly involved ex-Cabinet members, still under indictment. Several of the corporations have already been convicted. Public opinion has repudiated the use of "enemies" lists for harassment—political and otherwise.

Incidentally, in spite of the abuses, the percentage of the GNP represented in campaign contributions in recent elections has varied only from 0.00033 to 0.00037. The new Campaign Reform Act should take care of some of the abuses.

Bypassing Civil Service Commission regulations by requiring political clearance or making political appointments to positions not so designated seems to have been frequent. This is both illegal and unwise—and unnecessary. There are about 530 posts presently conceded to be political. There are also about 1,056 Schedule C positions which the commission has certified as eligible for political appointment, and another 530 noncareer positions around the President. The commission's approval is needed for a position to be allocated to Schedule C. Ambassadorial and certain other positions may be political if the President wishes, subject to Senate confirmation. The underlying questions (apart from legality) are whether the position is such that loyalty to the President's program must be assured, on the one hand; and, on the other, whether the desirability of retaining it in the career service is very much increased by making it one of those positions promotions to which act as a strong morale builder in the career service itself. Also, there is the question as to which would result in better service to the public.

There had been a new political tone in the Nixon administration in contrast to most recent Presidents. Regional officials were politicized; a layer of political appointees was introduced into OMB; there had been a wholesale replacement of the career Assistant Secretaries for Administration by policial appointees, and the politicization of many of those under them—in personnel, finance, budgeting, training, program evaluation. Many of these appointments were not illegal, but a product of insistence on agreement with the President's policies.

A considerable number of appointees were drawn from business, especially from advertising and public relations. It was alleged that many of them were unfamiliar with the difference between business and public service—ignoring both "public" and "service." Indoctrination as to their meaning was clearly lacking.

What are the future prospects for avoiding such a galaxy of abuses? Probably quite good, in part because of the laws already passed which have been mentioned; in part because it is now clear that courts can in general be relied upon and Presidents will obey them. Impeachment is workable, given sufficient provocation. It need not be and probably will not be used as a partisan device. Also the educational value of the exposures and the public reaction will probably, for a while at least, filter out candidates for President and key appointees who would constitute a menace to our system of government. Congress will be more alert. Perhaps a Congressional committee on intelligence, and provision for special prosecutors, may be enacted.

There are other restraints which apparently were effective with other Presidents, but not with Nixon. Such were the more frequent press conferences, the regular meetings with Congressional party leadership with which Nixon started but which lapsed toward the end, more access vouchsafed to Cabinet members. In the White House itself, there had been a more moderate tone of voice with most earlier Presidents, no tapes except for Lyndon Johnson who urged them upon Nixon, no overconfidence or arrogance or shortcuts because of a landslide victory. (FDR suffered some from this last-named.)

The public has been left with an exaggerated self-reproach—which may vanish now that the American system has proved that it works. No Constitutional amendment would appear to be needed.

We turn next to the strategy and tactics needed for better government in general, and for tempering the endemic evils of big government. In this sphere the policies and program of Richard Nixon look better.

NOTES

1. *Nixon was at least sure enough that they would be found correct to turn them over to Congress for inspection.

Chapter 18

The Federal System: Super Departments, White House Councils, Field Offices, Planning, Evaluation, Reorganization

Two alternative approaches face a President in formulating and presenting his program. Shall he attempt a massive and comprehensive legislative breakthrough, or shall he propose more incremental improvements?

After his landslide victory of 1972, Richard Nixon felt that the time had come for what he called a "revolution" on the domestic front. In his first term he had already executed what it is hoped will prove a massive breakthrough on the international scene. Could he now accomplish progress of a similar magnitude at home? Some of the main lines of his intent had already been foreshadowed. One of these which was potentially extremely important was executed under the reorganization procedure set up by Congress. This was the formation of the Domestic Council and the conversion of the Bureau of the Budget into the Office of Management and Budget. The first was designed in part to raise options as to what should be included in the President's domestic policy and program; the second was to advise as to how to put these into operation.

Two other factors should be borne in mind. The White House staff as organized and operating had come in for serious criticism on the basis of its size, fragmentation, and the addition to it of supervisory powers. The supervisory powers so placed were the subject of virtually unanimous adverse criticism at Airlie. Nixon had indicated, without being too explicit, that these attributes were not intended to be permanent, but would be greatly modified if his total, well-integrated program came into operation. The second factor was that he already had successful working models, which his total program would extend. These were principally four in number:

1. In the National Security Council, how to form policy without involving bureaucracy at the decision-making level, while using its expertise to develop options. This was hopefully to be repeated in the Domestic Council.

2. In the Department of Defense, how to organize more or less competitive units in such a fashion that the Secretary could (a) provide common services, (b) have tools to plan cooperation, reduce duplication, and otherwise integrate administratively distinct units around a common goal.

3. In the Domestic and National Security Councils, how to set up interdepartmental committees for overlapping functions, provide them with staff, and produce options for workable plans of cooperation and assignment of responsibilities.

4. In the shape of experience as to how *not* to do it, the existing organization of relations of the federal and state and local governments, including the way of meeting the financial needs of these latter.

Nixon attached great importance to a transfer of decision-making and program-planning to these state and local governments to the extent that this was practicable. Such a transfer would at one and the same time (a) reduce the size and complexity of the federal government, rendering more manageable what remained; (b) activate the interest and increase the discretion and control of the localities and states in their traditional and Constitutionally reserved functions of education, health, welfare, housing, land planning, community development, and many others presently covered by narrowly conceived categorical grants; (c) make possible greater adaptation to regional and local needs and conditions, minus the rigidity imposed by national standards and regulations; (d) head off the developing power brokerage between the functional people at the federal and state levels. As William Carey put it, "It amounts to off-loading peripheral, as well as contentious functions which are making a shambles of public management and satisfying not even the benefitting constituencies."[1]

Much of the shortfall on the part of the state and local governments in the functions in question had clearly been traceable to their inadequate revenues. The local units in particular had an inelastic system of taxation with its heavy reliance on the property tax. In certain instances, per capita taxable capacity varied by a factor of ten. Where the needs were greatest (in many of the central cities) the tax had already reached the point of being one of the factors driving out to the suburbs the middle class and the wealthy and much of the commerce and industry. Further tax increases were all too likely to be counterproductive by a further reduction of the central city's actual taxable capacity. There was also a vicious circle implicit in the criticism that the states and localities were to a considerable extent weak, irresponsible, and even corrupt. The history of the reform waves that had hit the cities in the past had indicated that the greater the responsibility and home rule, the more likely they were to be effective units, and the more civic interest they would arouse. The transfer of decisions to the national level implicit in the detailed grant system may well have exacerbated the low quality which lack of fiscal resources had produced. Probably in the transfer of discretion back again, a "lead time" of a year or two may be advisable for the smaller units to prepare for their new responsibilities and financing.

The central problem was met directly by proposals to transfer revenues under the heading of "revenue sharing." Clearly the nation had an interest, as did the

local units, in the functions in question. This had been the
basis for the early laws and subsidies for these functions.
Prior to the Great Depression of the 1930s the states and
localities had been making quite remarkable progress on
their own steam. With the depression came the fiscal
squeeze, and the federal government began to step into
the breach. Also from then on the nation continued to
preempt greater proportions of highly lucrative taxes.
These were or might have been otherwise available to the
smaller units: taxes on cigarettes, telephone and tele-
graph, amusements, liquor, income, gasoline.

Suggestions have been made that a better and more
responsible way of "general revenue sharing" than the
unearmarked grants now in effect would be to transfer
some of these taxes (for example, the cigarette tax)[2] to the
states—with the federal government aiding in its collection. The rate would be fixed in each instance as a part of
the state and local budgets, thereby strengthening their
fiscal responsibility.[3] Such a transfer was not a part of the
Nixon program.

The program was in two parts: general and special
revenue sharing. The first is in operation with the formula
taking need into account and providing that a substantial
portion should reach the local units. The state and local
units are asked to report the uses they made of it, but
otherwise there has been no nationwide stipulation other
than that it should be used in certain broad areas. The
principal questions raised concerning the plan have
involved local fiscal responsibility and the wisdom of the
actual uses made of the funds. Should the federal government retain some controls?

Special revenue sharing proposes the massive abolition
of the present detailed category grants (allegedly now
some 1,500), and their replacement by broadly functional
grants with the precise details as to use to be determined
locally. The only stipulation was that each broad grant
should be spent within the general orbit of its purpose,
education, health, land planning, mass transit, and so on.

Congress has already made some progress in the direction of consolidation of these category grants.

The issues raised are numerous. In the first place, the existing system is really too complex for the old departments to handle in its present form. Then, too, many of the antipoverty and other programs resulted in merely transferring the spoils to the ghettos. On the other hand, what would clearly result from special revenue sharing is a weakening of many of the existing subsystems nationally. The blacks especially feared the loss of power and in many instances, the loss of the "spoils" in the shape of their employment in the ghettos under the grants by category. The narrower groups of specialists among the functional people at all levels feared loss of power and employment. This would certainly hold true at the national level; it is part of the very purpose of the plan.

There should result a great simplification of procedures. This would also involve an abolition of much of the enormous paperwork both nationally and in the smaller units.

Ancillary to both the proposed devolution of responsibilities and the creation of super departments (to be described presently), has been the emergence of the Regional Councils. These have been briefly noted already, but they represent an important element in integration of the total program.

The first prerequisite is a continuation of the process of concentrating all relevant departmental field offices in one city in each region. The councils are expected to resolve an increasing number of interdepartmental and intradepartmental conflicts at this regional level. This would materially reduce the departmental congestion in Washington, and produce less special pleading at the White House level also. As at present, there would be a Presidential or Domestic Council or other Executive Office representative on each Regional Council. He would have the responsibility of interpreting Presidential policy and program, and consequently (within broad limits) of

command and control. He might well serve as chairman of
the council. This would weaken the subsystems, but
strengthen and clarify the Congressional role in broad
legislative determination of goals. The Presidential representatives could, if necessary, expedite action. As departments and bureaus are presently constituted, these
regional representatives of the White House are cutting
the bureaucratic lines to and from Washington. Under the
reorganized departments and the proposed functions of
the Domestic Council, this should be less and less
necessary. The regional representatives of the departments should have (a) demonstrated professional
competence; (b) executive ability to lead; (c) sympathy
with the philosophy of the President and the department
head. These qualifications can be required by their
Washington chief, on either their appointment or their
transfer to the regional assignment.

The third major sector of the Nixon program was to
have been a massive reshuffling of the departments and
agencies. The four inner departments—State, Treasury,
Defense, and Justice—were to be left largely intact.
Abolished as such were to be the primarily clientele-
oriented departments—Agriculture; Commerce; Labor;
Health, Education, and Welfare; Transportation; Housing and Urban Development; Interior. Also a certain
number of independent agencies, such as the Small Business Administration, and units of the Office of Economic
Opportunity of the Executive Office were to be incorporated into the larger plan. In place of the old departments and agencies, there would be established four goal-
oriented departments: Human Resources (mostly HEW),
Natural Resources (most of Interior and some of Agriculture), Community Development (built around HUD),
and Economic Affairs (Commerce, Labor, some of Agriculture, some of Transportation). The proposed internal
structure of these departments was also described. The
Secretary of each was to have a staff adequate to serve
him, including better management tools. "Administra-

tions" for each principal sector of the goal would concentrate on policy and program, with considerable emphasis on building the capabilities of their field structure. Planning units would be attached to the offices of the administrators, and not to the bureaus under them. The older, clientele-oriented departments had had such narrow missions that their very execution in programs was frustrated by conflicting missions of other narrowly oriented departments. Nor could they be depended on for broadly based policy ideas. Hence disputes and frustrations had been forced to the White House level. The clientele-oriented subsystems under the new plan would come in either at the administrator level or below. The interunit conflicts would be resolved, either by the administrator or the Secretary. Some of those units presently existing which had already been evaluated and found failing in the achievement of their objectives were to be administratively gutted, or eliminated from the President's budget. These shortcuts were to be used, even though the authorizing law was still on the statute books. In other words, no Congressional repeal was asked for. This was resented.

By resolving the conflicts within a proposed department, the White House need not concern itself with them. Remaining interdepartmental conflicts would go to the inner Presidency, presumably to the Domestic Council.

Thus Nixon proposed to go to the heart of the weakness in certain departments which had been a factor in his concentrating so much power in the White House. Defense, HEW, Transportation had not been pushed around. The first two were big enough and powerful enough to resolve most of their own conflicts. In any event, the President could not reasonably refuse to see their Secretaries. The White House did feel it had to get rid of the Secretary of Transportation by making him an ambassador, thus rendering the department more subservient.

Clearly the proposal challenged all kinds of vested interests in the subsystems, including Congress and the clienteles. The first breach was made by Agriculture, and this was so powerful that Nixon had to promise to retain the old department. Several committee chairmen opposed the Department of Community Development, but the Government Operations Committee under Congressman Chet Holifield voted to support it by a large majority. They felt that its formation would allow Congress a greater policy role by stimulating its concentration on the larger, goal-oriented issues. Opposition and criticism and some support were marshalling with regard to the other proposed Departments. But Watergate had taken over, and the whole plan was tabled. Yet these proposed departments met excellent criteria. They were to have a real responsibility for policy and program. They had a mission broad enough to be consistent with the public interest, and enough depth in jurisdiction so as to manage problems which must be cooperatively solved.

Meanwhile, in order to gain some of his objectives, Nixon announced a reorganization at the White House level. He reduced his immediate inner Cabinet to five: Kissinger (Foreign Affairs—State and Defense); Ehrlichman (Domestic Affairs), with three counselors, Natural Resources (Secretary of Agriculture), Human Resources (Secretary of HEW), Community Resources (Secretary of HUD); Schultz (Economic Affairs); Ash (Executive Branch Management); Haldeman (White House Operations). Only these five would have access to the President. The first four were to be his surrogates in their respective areas. The three counselors, Kissinger, and Ash would wear two hats and be physically housed in the White House or Executive Office. Whether Schulz would eventually become a superdepartment Secretary was unclear.

The whole temporary plan illustrated the atmosphere of unreality that had overtaken the White House. It was shortly withdrawn, and need not be discussed further. It was a desperate attempt on the part of Nixon to realize some of the objectives of his larger program in so far as he had the apparent authority "on his own." It clearly overshot the mark and helped to kill the plans themselves for the time being.

The fourth major step had in part already been taken. This was the establishment of the Domestic Council. If and when the original design was completed, the inner Presidency would consist of a greatly reduced White House staff, an Executive Office cleared of minor agencies, the Office of Management and Budget, the Council of Economic Advisers, and two other major councils, the National Security and the Domestic, which latter two the President himself might chair or he might constitute the Vice-President or the staff director of each as his alter ego on occasions. Under the directors, who would probably be subject to confirmation by the Senate, would be staffs of experts. These experts from time to time would be assigned to interdepartmental committees, either *ad hoc* or permanent, as need directed. The Secretaries of the appropriate departments would be members of one or both of the parent councils; or, if not regular members of the other council, could sit in on occasion. The Director of OMB would be a member of both, and the NSC would in general remain as at present.

The Domestic Council would eventually be reduced in size, with the consolidation of the old departments. Probably the Veterans Administration would remain as an independent agency, and at least initially its head would be a member of the Domestic Council. The Vice-President would also probably remain a member of both.

Like the NSC, the DC was expected to function largely through a flexible network of interdepartmental committees staffed from the council's staff. As yet it has scarcely gotten off the ground. Its proposed functions, including access to the President, a forum for interdepartmental concerns, development of program options, and sponsoring evaluations, are important. At least some of these would appear to be better performed through this medium than through either an unwieldy Cabinet or the OMB. The Cabinet in its original form would probably largely fade out, except when the President occasionally desired to brief it on some important matter or as a ceremonial ornament to appear in public or be photographed. The Domestic Council clearly would work better with fewer and larger departments, which had presumably sufficiently wide orbit to limit the agenda of the DC. It would take several years to consolidate its role and maximize its usefulness.

The case for the major proposals is that they speak to the following problems: (a) bigness and complexity, (b) democratic participation, (c) economy (at least at the federal level, (d) adaptability to local conditions, (e) interface and conflict, (f) manageability, (g) lessened clientele pressure, (h) facilitating evaluation of programs in terms of goals and priorities, (i) control of the bureaucracy. It is difficult to imagine a stronger case, or one more to the point.

There were at least some immediate though temporary unfortunate effects, such as the creation of a vast number of uncertainties, especially in the career service. This was most noticeable in the "principalities" that had been built around the category grants. Further tensions resulted from what some saw to be an extension of the powers granted to the inner Presidency. There was also great concern in other quarters for fear that Nixon would not really try to follow through.

The oppositon was strong, and regardless of Watergate might well have proved fatal.

In the first place, the proposal would disturb Congressional ways, especially in confusing existing committee and subcommittee powers.

In the second place, clienteles would fight it—both big and small. They do not like to disturb their cozy subsystem whirlpool relationships.

Finally, policy determination, including organization, is thought of by Congress as ultimately resting in its legis-

lative and appropriating functions. Will it accept a clari-
fying and facilitating of its role in the greater decisions, in
lieu of lessening its present detailed relations with the
bureaus?

The conferees at Airlie were not so much opposed to
the rationalization of departmental structure as they were
in thinking that the opposition—congressional and clientele—was simply too formidable. Any reorganization, as
Congress knew, was bound to affect policy. It would also
redistribute power.

Nixon at least raised some basic issues. Quite possibly all
future discussions of any consequence on our federal
government as a whole will now have to take them into
account. All previous commissions and task forces in this
area had recommended both fewer and goal-oriented
departments. Someday a less vulnerable President may
make them part of his program, or perhaps Congress may
concern itself from time to time with one or another of the
items. Consolidation of grants in one or more of the
areas, a firmer establishment of the Domestic Council,
reorganization which brings in one of the goal-oriented
departments are distinct possibilities. The first of these
has been partially accomplished.

On the other hand, the report of the National Academy
to the Ervin Committee arising out of Watergate spoke in
favor of a pluralistic model in the Executive Branch to
respond to the pluralistic structure of the Congressional
committees.

Nixon himself was a strange mixture. Moynihan
credited him with unusual insights, and this is correct. No
one who reads his program as a whole can fail to recognize
these elements of potential greatness. Then—when one
turns to the debacle and circumstances of his resignation;
to his overreaction to opposition, especially to
demonstrations and riots; to the cavalier fashion with
which he dealt with laws, Congress, the career service—an
element of great tragedy emerges, the tragedy of a great
failure.

Leaving aside Nixon and his programs, we turn to the more modest suggested incremental improvements in the functioning of the Presidency. The list is a long one: many surfaced in the discussion at Airlie. Some are mutually exclusive. By no means would all of them be approved with anything that would approach unanimity or even a majority. Many have been treated already in the earlier chapters.[4] A few are singled out for discussion here.

Because it figured so largely at Airlie, and because it has been a recurrent theme in this book, we shall start with the need for more long-range planning. There was universal agreement at Airlie as to the need, but difference of opinion as to where precisely it should be located. The discussion itself centered largely on the pros and cons of and aternatives to the proposal made by Rufus Miles in 1967, that the "Office of Policy Studies" be located in the White House, or at least in the inner Presidency. It would report only to the President. It would be adequately staffed, mostly by people borrowed from the agencies, with a certain number brought in from outside the government. The staff should not testify before Congress nor should confirmation by the Senate be required. Its principal function would be as a "think tank" or sensitive analytic body to identify ahead of time potential crises and opportunities. In the economic field, it would be a kind of long-range Council of Economic Advisers. In the social and governmental and international field, it would presumably have reported to the President matters such as the crisis in the central cities or the world food shortage. Especially important would be its identification of social trends with their dangers and possibilities. Some comments on the plan accepted it as, in effect, a distinct body with the functions as proposed, but would locate it either in the OMB or more directly in connection with the Domestic Council and the NSC, or as an adjunct to a new body proposed to (but rejected by) President Johnson, called the Office of Policy Development. In any event the departments might sabotage its recommendations. One person feared it might "cop out" by shielding a President from unpleasant news. An alleged reason for the departure of the science advisers from the White House was their tendency to give advice which the President did not wish to hear. Others advocated scattering the planning among the departments, saying that only planning directly related to ongoing programs would really be relevant. This would be especially effective, if the departments were to become goal-oriented. One conferee placed his faith in *ad hoc*-ery—in other words, in task forces set up from time to time to forecast the future. The commission set up by Nelson Rockefeller as a private venture on his retirement as Governor of New York might serve as a model.

It was brought out in the course of the discussion that, while the old National Resources Planning Board had been done to death by its enemies, it did produce a number of eventually influential studies. Urbanism, economic stabilization, budgeting for countercyclical timing were among these.

The war spawned many planning agencies, with the Economic Stabilization Act of 1946 one of the results. The National Security Council and the Office of Emergency Planning were other offshoots. Some long-range planning is in fact taking place today, but it is scattered in many places. All agreed that had such planning as that under discussion actually existed, government improvisation with its contributions to the "credibility gap" would have been greatly lessened. Environmental degradation, the strangling of the central cities, the unsatisfactory nature of education, the scarcity of resources were all cited as examples.

The responses by the advocates of a separate White House unit were predictable and impressive. Planning that now exists in the separate departments assumes the continuation of their existing responsibilities. It is useful, but limited. Even such long-range planning efforts as potentially exist in the agencies presently located in the

Executive Office are largely sluiced off in favor of attention to immediate concerns. One danger in all long-range planning is that the immediate political consequences of the best option would be fatal. Special task forces were hazardous in their timing. On the other hand, a permanent planning presence in the White House could help greatly by advance thinking about policy goals, especially those with interdepartmental aspects. Nor would this necessarily be incompatible with the retention of planning units in the offices of a department secretary.

Closely related to planning is the determination of national priorities. The constraints of the budget are very great. About half of it is virtually predetermined by laws now on the books. Social security, veterans' benefits, government pensions, grants to states and localities under commitments appearing in formulas (especially in the federal highway program), interest on the debt are fixed, unless there are some drastic changes in the laws—changes which as of today do not appear to be politically practicable. Some would include the great bulk defense expenditures as similarly inviolate. Under the latest agreement with the Soviet they are probably to be increased substantially unless the Soviet and we can come to some agreement other than a ceiling limiting the extent of the increase. As of the present time the costs of just about everything are going up, while the heart of the tax base, which is productivity, is more or less static.

In a sense the series of impoundments by Nixon were fulfilling an evaluation role as he saw it. So also was the omission of provision for certain legally mandated functions in his last budget. Presumably these impoundments and omissions were worked out in the inner Presidency, with OMB and the White House staff playing a leading role. The Ford budget is yet to be acted upon, but even the $4 to $5 billion savings proposed for the current year have not proved practicable. Many were in the form of postponements. Congress has already overridden Ford's veto on increased veterans' benefits and some other quite costly matters. Some of the economies allegedly effected by the appropriations committees in the past have been in the form of second-guessing the departments or the OMB on the probable costs of mandatory expenditures. The cuts have later been largely rescinded in supplemental or deficiency appropriations bills.

Current crises—inflation, energy, major unemployment—are rightly being used as occasions for soul-searching as regards national priorities. As in the past, presumably the OMB is preparing options, and the Congressional leadership and its budget committees are working on the legislative and appropriations fronts. Inexorably this leads to a process relatively new in our governmental activity, the evaluation of existing functions.

Evaluation would seem to be a commonsense necessity in the determination of priorities, yet it has been sparingly used in the past. The old BOB and OMB examiners and the Appropriations committees in Congress have customarily of late—during our presumed continuation of the steady growth in the GNP—largely taken for granted past activities at their existing levels, and concentrated on requests for staff additions. PPBS (Planning-Programming-Budgeting Systems) was a noble attempt to force a justification for these—including existing expenditure and staffing levels. Some efforts have been made to relate costs over the years to productivity levels in terms of units of output, but many of these have been defeated by bureaucratic legerdemain adept in changing the basis of comparison. It is somewhat standard practice for agencies to single out some popular activity for a cutback if a percentage cut is imposed, relying on clientele pressure to force a restoration. This restoration often happens at the Senate appropriations review stage. There is also an alleged practice whereby an agency inserts in its budget certain optional expenditures—desirable, but not necessary, thereby allowing the appropriations committees to make a show of economy by cutting them out. The committees and their staffs are adept at recognizing these.

The Congressional budget is in its first year, and its effects are uncertain.

Congressional investigations also take the place of activities unpopular in certain quarters. The General Accounting Office is a new and powerful tool in this regard, in conducting such evaluations.

In the Executive Branch it is expected that the OMB's role in program evaluation will be increased significantly. Evaluation of a departmental function itself is more difficult; but if goal-oriented departments are established, they would be an appropriate medium at the level of the office of the Secretary. It is probable, for example, that the cost-benefit calculations of the great water resource construction agencies are highly vulnerable. We may well be running out of justifiable projects for the Corps of Engineers and the Bureau of Reclamation. There is also an unresolved interface between values connected with the the environment and the construction of many interstate highways, notably the sector that would add to urban congestion.

However, there is presently no real *center* for systematic reevaluations in terms of either obsolescence, non-fulfillment of objectives, or national priorities. The most recent systematic reevaluation has been of the activities of the Office of Economic Opportunity, partly by the agency itself—where a new team was sent in for the purpose. It was Nixon's intention to transfer to existing agencies the functions which had proved themselves worthy, and by one means or another to phase out the remainder.

Either the OMB or the Domestic Council or a high-powered *ad hoc* task force would appear to be appropriate vehicles for re-evaluation. Either of the first two could establish an effective continuing unit, given the will and the wherewithal. The GAO is serving as a Congressional alternative. The OMB is presently attempting this, but on an inadequate scale.

There remain a number of possible reorganizations of the national government, apart from the Nixon program and others already mentioned. Without going into detail, most are concerned with a few objectives: providing more comprehensive goal-oriented departments, dividing existing departments or combining certain agencies to create a new department, moving some function into the Executive Office so as to give it more attention or prestige, moving some function or bureau from one department to another to promote better intergration.

Reorganization can be a most useful tool. It can also be a way of downgrading or perhaps ultimately getting rid of a function, or alternatively catering to a particular clientele by upgrading the function even to the departmental level. From time to time there will be reorganizations, especially if the supple tool is restored, whereby a President can propose, subject only to one form or another of Congressional veto or endorsement.

With this we leave the future. Clearly major changes in the Institutional Presidency lie ahead. We may hope that it will prove as adaptable and as supple as in certain periods in the past. May further adaptations be not too long delayed.

NOTES

1. William D. Carey, "New Perspective on Governance," in the Conference Board, *Challenge to Leadership: Managing in a Changing World* (New York: Free Press, 1973), p. 69.

2. This suggestion has been made by Frank Bane, formerly executive secretary of the Council of State Governments.

3. Tax stamps of the state and/or locality would be affixed at the factory by the federal government; sales and delivery would be restricted accordingly.

4. A list of these will be found in Appendix B.

Chapter 19

Epilogue: Advice to a President

The Institutional Presidency remains the operating center of our national government. If it falters, the nation is shaken. If it is strong, the nation will gain confidence.

Over 140 recommendations have been recounted in this study.[1] In large part, they were those presented in the papers and discussions at the Airlie conference. Most of them concerned changes in organization and procedure.

Organization and procedure cannot take the place of the quality of the men in key posts. They can, however:

1. Make participation more attractive to good men;
2. Release their potentials;
3. Improve accountability;
4. Interrelate separately administered activities;
5. Improve communication and understanding;
6. Facilitate more intelligent decisions. Under this heading the importance of the President and the other decision-makers having options developed for their key choices has been a recurrent theme.

At this point, we shall repeat, in summarized form, some of the most important recommendations.

For the most part, the National Security Council and the Domestic Council should assume the traditional functions of Cabinet meetings. The President will be sensitive to certain great questions or briefings for which the larger body is more appropriate.

The President should appoint strong men and women of integrity to head the departments and agencies and as members of the regulatory commissions. Once they have been appointed and confirmed by the Senate, he should confidently entrust to them the administration and program of their respective units. He should rely on their participation in the NSC and the DC, their own perceptions, and his staff monitors to identify important problems, especially those of an interdepartmental nature.

They should appoint their assistants, subject to his veto. They should each organize a small staff, not connected with any of their bureaus, to aid them in budget, personnel, Congressional relations, development of program, long-range and goal-oriented planning evaluations.

These heads should insist that all their departmental and agency activities be carefully coordinated with the President's goals, and with efforts on the part of his staff in Congressional and press relations.

They should learn how to work with and seek the aid of the senior career service.

Heads of departments and agencies should have direct access to the President.

The President should hold regular or frequent meetings with the NSC and DC, and with the Congressional leadership.

Most social problems and much potential interdepartmental coordination are in the field. The President should take steps to recognize this.

The President must be on constant guard against the isolation and insulation that come with power. Hence he will structure into his procedures the "adversary relationship." Congress and the press can be especially helpful in this regard.

Congress is to a great extent accustomed to specialize along pluralistic lines. The value to the nation of the vitality of the various groups and clienteles so represented, and their counterparts in the Executive Branch, is very great. Coordination and release of these vitalities that are not contrary to the greater national interest are twin objectives. Congress may itself aid the President in this.

Press conferences should be as the President sees fit. They should average at least once a month. Television talks to the nation are important at critical moments.

At the heart of our federal system is the question of the respective roles of our national and our state and local governments. This is two-pronged. What should each do, and how should the financing be divided? There is very considerable support for transfer of funds under general and special revenue sharing. Accompanying the latter there would be a massive consolidaion of 1,500 or so special category grants into a few major grants for funcions traditionally associated with the states and local units. Within the funds broadly earmarked for a function such as education, health, housing, the states and local units would have complete freedom of use according to their own needs as they see them. This would greatly simplify and reduce the cost for personnel in the federal government and would enormously enlarge the scope of state and local self-government. This process has begun.

The final note of the conference was that a President should "go to it and be the biggest man he can." The support for a strong Presidency was unanimous. There was an equal belief that Congress should be strong.[2] The genius of our Constitution is best expressed when the Presidency and Congress are *both* strong—with both motivated by the public interest and ready basically to cooperate each with the other. They would employ their respective checks, only when their differing perceptions cause differences in the dictates of their conscience and intelligence.

Again and again—at Airlie, and wherever the Presidency is discussed in depth—the question recurs, "What do we expect a President to do and be?"

I

He will operate in accord with the genius of our Constitution. In other words, he will perform his function strongly, but as a member of a team which has two players—himself and Congress. These ought to respect each other, and each play a distinctive role. He must be responsible—in that he must expect to justify what he does before Congress, his Constitutional equal. He must keep within the bounds as determined by the judiciary. He will be ready to give reasons for his actions. He will be sparing in his claims of executive privilege. He will operate within the laws and the intent of Congress in passing these laws. Where these laws have given him discretion, and where the Constitution has endowed him with the power to conduct foreign relations and to command the armed services, he will consult with the Congressional leadership, informing them of his principal actions and goals, and asking their support and understanding.

II

He will develop a program in which he exercises leadership but not compulsion—toward the goals and for the solution of the problems of the nation and the world as he sees them, including generations still to come as well as of the present day. He will work toward this program in cooperation with other bodies: Congress, his staff and the Executive Office, his political appointees, the career service, the states and localities, other nations, the press and media, the political parties, the groups (ethnic, economic, public interest), the public. He will be sensitive to the objectives of these other groups, cooperating with them in so far as he feels this to be in the public interest.

He will fly "trial balloons" in certain important goals concerning which he has options as to means. He will be especially sensitive to long-range effects of his intended proposals. He will have so organized his White House staff and Executive Office that at all stages save his final decision he may have both political and expert input. In the end, he will make his own decisions.

He will then orchestrate the development of support for his program.

He will again meet with the party leadership of Congress immediately after his "State of the Union," Economic Report, and budget messages—asking for both support and identification of problems. His department heads and appropriate members of his staff will take further Congressional soundings on particular items and on the program as a whole.

With the department and agency heads, he will operate initially through the NSC and DC, asking for reactions, making assignments, asking for ideas for his press conference on the program, identifying interdepartmental problems, himself making suggestions for enlisting the support of their top political and career associates.

He will hold a press conference as soon as he has been briefed by the departments as to probable questions. This will be televised over national network for maximum public impact.

In so far as his program involves cooperation with other nations in joint goals, he will have informed the nations involved before he delivers his message, and discovered the mood in which his proposals will be received. After the message, he will activate the State Department for further negotiations, looking toward one or more "summit" conferences or an addresss to the United Nations, if wisdom dictates.

If initial reactions are favorable, he will arrange to address the governors' conference and appropriate forums to reach the cities and rural areas. Regional or functional speaking engagements should be sought for members of the Cabinet.

During all this process, his associates should be in constant contact with appropriate Congressional committees and their staffs. If minor changes would improve the chances for a bill, he should be ready to accommodate. If some important item of his program is in trouble, but probably could be salvaged, he may address the nation. If Congress gives him a bill that is in the general direction of his goals, and he has been unable to secure all the changes he wanted in transit, he will normally sign it—but point out the weaknesses and the "unfinished business."

III

He will administer a vast governmental body, moving it in the direction of its being so organized as best to influence its action in the public good, to release its cooperative potential, to see that clear options are produced to reach national goals, to select from these options (so far as lies within his power and influence) those most calculated to achieve these goals. In its current operation, he will stress that best use of resources, by evaluation of programs already in operation, by long range planning, by efficient and economical processes, by cooperation between the various units. He will be impatient with undue delays, ruthless with sabotage, resolute in dealing with those who put private interest ahead of public good.

He will inherit a government with both strengths and weaknesses. In many instances the weaknesses are merely areas not yet reached by the strengths.

For example, the process of generating foreign policy has been remarkably successful in certain areas. Can the same methods be applied to the remaining areas?

How far are the methods used in foreign policy adaptable to domestic policy?

The successes in foreign policy have been in those areas of greatest immediate importance—Soviet relations, mainland China, arms limitation, progress toward a Middle East settlement. Those that have now come to be of comparable importance are the arrested development in Western European community cooperation, world inflation, the energy crisis and its backfire in economic instability, the world food and population crisis. Our own future is deeply involved in all of these, as well as in further steps in the still fragile successes in the areas noted before.

There are also a number of areas which only by comparison seem minor. They have suffered from lack of attention because of lack of time on the part of the principal operators. They should not so suffer. The Secretary of State can designate teams to handle them, checking with him only as to the final option preferred by the team.

The elements in the successes to date have been identified, and should be applied to the unfinished business.[3]

With adaptations, a similar method can be used for domestic problems. The Domestic Council will perform the role of the NSC. Its staff director could also serve as the President's chief assistant for domestic affairs. DSM's (Domestic Study Memoranda) will ferret out the options. Review boards will be more *ad hoc* than in the NSC. If interdepartmental relations are involved, a board should have a chairman from the President's staff, the OMB, or the CEA. When the findings and the options reach the President, he will incorporate his decision in a binding memo to the principal actors.

Less important matters may be handled by the review board, with the memo presumably drafted by the chairman, but issued over the signature, either of the President or the department head or heads involved. If agreement cannot be reached, the President will have to make the final decision, or table the matter for the time being.

It should be noted that as at present constituted, the Domestic Council is a very large and perhaps somewhat unwieldy body. If a departmental reorganization ever succeeds in replacing a number of the departments, the DC would be smaller and more effective. It would also have fewer problems, as many more could be worked out within the confines of a single department. In any event, it will continue to work largely through committees, permanent and *ad hoc*, armed with adequate staff.

Another important shortcoming in the organization of the government is the absence of any effective unit for long-range planning. Such a unit is most easily created in the Executive Office of the President, but there are alternatives.[4]

Evaluation mechanisms are at present seriously deficient as regards our existing functions. Probably the OMB or a special task force is the best medium, as self-analyses are likely to be self-serving. Priorities must take old as well as new functions into account.[5] The General Accounting Office, operating under a Congressional mandate, may be the best evaluator of all.

His own White House staff needs an inner logic. There are potential and actual elements of great strength. If the NSC and DC are continued, as they should be, his chief assistants for the national security and the domestic concerns respectively can be placed in charge of staff units in the Executive Office to service these two bodies. Experience will almost certainly show that more than one assistant is needed for domestic concerns, and these assistants can serve as staff directors along functional lines—e.g., Natural Resources, Economics, Human Resources, Community Development. They need no power other than to direct the staffs, but the President may wish to have them confirmed by the Senate. The CEA are so confirmed, and this has presented no problems.

Apart from these assistants (three to six in number), the President will clearly need a number of "monitors" to see that the directives issued in various matters are in fact operating. (It is assumed that the staff directors will see that deadlines are met by their staffs in the preparation of the NSSM's and the DSM's, and that the review boards are duly scheduled, and so on. An overall coordinator may be needed for this, if the load is too heavy.)

The monitors who may or may not deal exclusively with particular departments can also carry out other inquiries for the President.

The President will also need two or more press secretaries, a Congressional relations unit, which in some instances will coordinate its work with the departmental

Assistant Secretaries for Congressional Relations (a unit of
one or more), perhaps a Science Adviser, and one or two
assistants to deal with the state and local governments.

The total of active, responsible assistants would appear
to be about twenty-five. In addition there will be fairly
substantial staff for the NSC and the DC, located in the
Executive Office. Many of these latter will be specialists
detailed from departments on *ad hoc* assignments.[6]

He will also have a long-range planning unit, the OMB,
the CEA, perhaps the CEQ, and such other units as he or
Congress may wish to assign to the Executive Office for
temporary White House direction. The present number
should almost certainly be reduced, and the device itself
sparingly used in the future.[7]

He does not exercise these functions single-handed. He
has vast potential in the way of assistance at every point.
Yet in all matters vital to the nation, he must make the
final decision as to means and ends, insofar as his power
and influence extend. In the words of President Truman,
"The buck stops here."

IV

He will, by example, image, and appeal, try as best he
can to lead in the ideals and traditions of the past, and be
sensitive to national missions that lie ahead. He will try to
unify the people around these national missions so as to
realize the dreams of a way of life for the United States
that (among other goals) will allow each strand of our
variety of cultures to make its own constructive
contribution. He will be President of *all* the people.

He should be steeped in our national history and
traditions. He will thereby recognize the elements of
greatness in our greatest Presidents—Washington, Jeffer-
son, Lincoln, the two Roosevelts, Wilson, and Truman.

He should also recognize the conflicting, confusing, and
dangerous elements in our contemporary society and the
world at large—and the elements of promise. He must

"navigate through the tricky tides of shifting values and ethics, and often quickly seize fleeting opportunities."[8] With deep understanding of all of these, with a combination of determination and humility as God gives him to see the right, he will be the biggest man he can be, adding to his own strength the strength of others who like him would recapture a sense of mission for our people.

NOTES

1. See Appendix B.
2. In another volume the author has dealt at length with Congress, its usages, its potential, the forces that beset and inspire it. See Ernest S. Griffith and Francis Valeo, *Congress: Its Contemporary Role*, 5th Ed., rev. (New York: New York University Press, 1975).
3. See pp. 64–66.
4. See pp. 202 ff.
5. See pp. 205–206.
6. See Chapter 2.
7. See Chapter 3.
8. Griffith and Valeo, *Congress*, p. 64.

Appendix A

Participants
The Airlie Conference on the
Institutional Presidency
April 11–13, 1974

William I. Bacchus
Staff Member
Commission on the Organization of The Government
for the Conduct of Foreign
Policy

Samuel H. Beer
Professor of Government
Harvard University

David E. Bell
Executive Vice President
The Ford Foundation

Shawn Bernstein
Project Assistant
Committee for Economic
Development

William M. Capron
Assistant Dean
John F. Kennedy School
of Government
Harvard University

Lisle C. Carter
Chancellor
Atlanta University Center

Frederic N. Cleaveland*
Chairman
National Academy of Public
Administration

John J. Corson
Consultant
National Academy of Public
Administration

Roy W. Crawley
Executive Director
National Academy of Public
Administration

Alan L. Dean
Vice President-Administration
U.S. Railway Association

Lyle C. Fitch
President
Institute of Public
Administration

William T. Golden
Corporate Director and
Trustee
New York, New York

218

Kermit Gordon*
President
The Brookings Institution

George A. Graham
Senior Social Scientist
National Academy of Public
  Administration

Sam Halper
Former Contributing Editor
and Caribbean Bureau Chief
  Time Magazine

Roger W. Jones
Consultant
National Academy of Public
  Administration

Robert F. Lenhart
Vice President-adminis-
  tration
  Committee for Economic
  Development

James S. Lipscomb
Executive Director
The George Gund
  Foundation

Robert E. Merriam*
Chairman
Advisory Commission on
  Intergovernmental
  Relations

Rufus E. Miles, Jr.
Former Assistant Secretary
Department of Health,
  Education, and Welfare

Frederick C. Mosher
Doherty Professor of
Government and Foreign
  Affairs
  University of Virginia

Richard E. Neustadt*
Associate Dean
John F. Kennedy School of
  Government
  Harvard University

Harold Orlans
Senior Research Associate
National Academy of Public
  Administration

Don K. Price (Conference
  Chairman)*
Dean
John F. Kennedy School of
  Government
  Harvard University

Herbert Roback
Staff Director
House Committee on
  Government Operations

James H. Rowe, Jr.
Attorney
Washington, D.C.

Eileen Shanahan
Washington Bureau
New York Times

Theodore C. Sorensen
Paul, Weiss, Rifkind,
Wharton and Garrison
  New York, New York

Elmer B. Staats
Comptroller General of the
United States

James L. Sundquist
Senior Fellow
The Brookings Institution

Wayne E. Thompson*
Member, Board of Trustees
Committee for Economic
  Development

Robert C. Weaver
Distinguished Professor of
  Urban Affairs
  Hunter College

ACADEMY STAFF

Richard L. Chapman,
  Project Director

Carol Neill

Carla Starkey

Claire Tepper

*Chairman of Conference Session

Appendix B

Recommendations for the Institutional Presidency

These are largely assembled from the text. The majority were voiced at the Airlie Conference, with varying degrees of support. In some instances, they represent a voicing by only one particpant, but with no negatives in response. Others are ones not discussed at the Conference, but which appear in writings on the Presidency.

In each instance, I have attempted to indicate the apparent degree of support, including both the Conference and writings as the basis for classification. Such indication is by letters or symbols as follows:

> U = apparent unanimity.
> F = favorable reaction. Some dissent.
> ? = sentiment fairly evenly divided.
> N = largely negative. Some favorable.

I have also marked * the ones deemed most important. These judgments are necessarily subjective. The headings are somewhat arbitrary.

GENERAL

? Parties no longer have much meaning in issue orientations.

N   The direct primary has rendered issue-oriented national parties obsolete in congressional elections.

?   Presidents should reward the most able party workers by appointing them to key positions, in preference to career men.

?   Whether a stronger party system will give more attention to the powerless than otherwise was subject to differing answers.

?   Establish an ombudsman as a channel for grievances.

U   Too much material is classified.

F   De-classification should be greatly widened. (n.b. The expense involved was regarded as the principal barrier.)

U   Transitions between presidencies should be perfected.

?   Withdraw altogether from "black activities" by intelligence agencies.

U   Do not use IRS records for political purposes.

U*   No Constitutional Amendment is needed relevant to the Institutional Presidency.

U*   National priorities must be determined in some better way than at present. This determination must include evaluations of existing functions. Alternative instruments for evaluations are numerous.

THE PRESIDENT

U* Retain suppleness in thinking about interrelationships in our government.

F* The President should concern himself largely with political responsibility (i.e. with policy), for the most part leaving managerial efficiency to the departments.

U* In preparing his program the President should seek the aid of Cabinet members and the "inner presidency". This could be on request and/or through the NSC and DC.

U The President should not attempt to abolish authorized functions by omitting them in his budget.

? The President should not "overuse" his veto.

U A President should be cautious in his use of executive privilege.

U* A President should not use unspecified emergency powers without at least subsequent notification to or validation of, by Congress.

U* A President should feel himself primarily as an exponent of the national or public interest.

U* A President must be on constant guard against the isolation that threatens any one in a position of power. He must encourage and institutionalize adversary opinions.

U* A President should have a program, and stay with the main elements in it, unless situations change. It should be incorporated for the most part in the annual "State of the Union" messages.

F* In making decisions in foreign policy, the President must be ready at some stage in the process to submit his probable decisions to informed criticism. There are many channels available for this, including congressional intimations to the press.

U* The President must make the ultimate foreign policy decisions, subject to the Constitutional powers of Congress.

F* Presidents should always have a vehicle to develop options in important decisions as to program and policy. Unless a department is goal-oriented and has an internal structure which will develop such options, it must be outside the department affected.

F   Use agency rivalries constructively, with reorganization, a back-up tool.

U   External task forces or commissions may from time to time be used to develop ideas for the President's program.

U* The President must have a method for handling interdepartmental problems, over-lap and duplication, jurisdictional disputes, conflict, failures in cooperation, and integration of effort.

?   A President running for reelection should be ready to debate his opponent.

F   Programs are best at the integrating level of clientele conflicts.

F   In appointments to the regulatory commissions, presidents should select nominees who hold the public interest dominant, and who have no clientele orientation.

U   A President should investigate all key appointments for potential conflicts of interest, before sending nominations to the Senate.

U* There should be certain bodies with which the President should meet regularly: the NSC and the DC (both in lieu of the Cabinet), the press, the congressional leadership.

U   Do not let a landslide victory tempt a President to "cut corners."

U   A President should have an adequate information system.

U* Either options or an "adversary" relationship should be available in all important decisions including intelligence estimates.

U* Beware in advance of possible bias, derived from loyalty to one's agency or clientele.

U* Avoid those attitudes in dealing with advisers that encourage "Yes men."

U   Executive privilege is justified in inter-office memos or taped conversations, during the discussion process prior to a decision.

N   Give the President an item veto. This can probably be done by an Act of Congress, but it may require a Constitutional Amendment.

THE WHITE HOUSE STAFF

F* If surrogate roles are assigned to persons on the White House staff and in the Executive Office, they should be confirmed by Congress, and be ready to appear before congressional committees. In general, it is unwise to assign in this fashion or to interpose them between the President and members of the Cabinet.

U* The President should use his staff to monitor the

departments and agencies to make certain his directives are carried out.

N* Create the office of Assistant President (for administration?).

?* Do not use the "two hats" method.

F Reduce the size of the White House staff.

U* The White House Assistant for National Security should be kept informed of the less important foreign policy decisions.

U* There should be a high level National Security Assistant on the White House staff.

U Do not allow the White House staff to preempt access to the President.

U* Assignment of tasks to White House staff and others should be explicit, with provision for follow-up if necessary.

F Staff layering between the President and department heads should be avoided.

N "Two hat" men should also have two desks.

? There should be on the White House staff at least two persons of the Bundy-Sorenson type—one foreign, one domestic—to assist the President directly on interdepartmental affairs. They must work closely with the NSC and DC.

F The President's own staff must not be larger than he can personally deal with. They must be able to think institutionally, as well as having a subject matter expertise.

F   If a President unilaterally delegates power to assistants not subject to Senate confirmation, he cannot disavow their acts.

THE EXECUTIVE OFFICE
(including the National Security and Domestic Councils)

F* Actively use the NSC.

F* Retain the Domestic Council, and develop its functions as proposed.

N* Move the Civil Service Commission into the Executive Office. (some sentiment for revamping or dividing the functions of the Commission).

U   Tidy up the Executive Office, by removing those agencies not clearly relevant to the "inner presidency."

?   If surrogate roles are assigned to persons or units in the "inner presidency," put them under a Cabinet member "without portfolio."

F* Options should be developed before all major decisions in foreign policy.

F* These options should be related to long-range, established goals, preferably using the NSSM method.

F* The principal actors should — if time and security allow — have the opportunity to participate in the formulation of these options.

F* In general, the State Department (and not the White House Staff) should play the lead role in foreign policy.

U* A machinery should be set up to identify inconsistencies in policy decisions and to see that they are resolved in terms of goal priorities.

F* Retain the Washington Special Action Group (or a similar body) to handle crisis situations quickly.

U* Use interdepartmental committees from the NSC and DC rather than from the Cabinet as such, because they can then be staffed.

N Create an Office of Program Development.

U* Long range planning should take place in important fields.

?* This is best accomplished by a unit in the Executive Office, or on the White House staff. It may be departmental or by task forces.

F Its membership should not require confirmation, nor should they give testimony before Congress.

F* An independent evaluating mechanism must be institutionalized in the Executive Office, along with subsidiaries in goal-oriented departments.

U* Staff is needed to develop options. These may be in the "inner presidency" or associated with goal-oriented departments.

U* Interdepartmental committees, equipped with staff, represent the best way to develop options in grappling with interdepartmental problems. The assignment of such responsibility to the OMB is a viable option, especially if the OMB will be certain to consult the departments involved. So also is assignment to the NSC or DC.

F* If the Domestic Council is chosen as the primary source for interdepartmental committees, its staff must be greatly enlarged and diversified to provide the necessary competency to staff these committees. So must the OMB, if that is the President's choice.

N Rehabilitate the Legislative Reference unit in the OMB as an alternative to the DC for interdepartmental problems.

THE CABINET AND AGENCIES

U*Cabinet members should have access to the President.

U*Strengthen the staff of a Department Secretary.

U*Comprehensive, goal-oriented departments can — if the Secretary is equipped with adequate, competent staff — do a better job at monitoring their own bureaus, than can the clientele-oriented departments.

U*The political chief and the top career men in a unit should understand each other's position and views, and seek the maximum cooperation within the limits set by Congress.

U* Frequent and candid contacts within a department on the part of the political and the career men should take place as to the goals of a given unit and the options for attaining them. (See the tentative model in Chapter VIII).

U The political chiefs should identify within their units those career men who have in the past been through executive training programs or internships or educational leave. They constitute a useful nucleus for promotions as need may arise.

N More frequent use of the Cabinet.

D Appoint stronger members to the Cabinet.

F Use a career man as Assistant Secretary for Administration.

U*A Cabinet member should choose his own Assistant and Under Secretaries, subject to the President's veto.

U* Key political appointees should have an orientation program.

U* Cabinet members should assume more responsibility in their departments.

U* Cabinet members should listen to and use the top career men.

F* Find the top career men in an agency who will cooperate with their head in introducing the president's program, and use them.

?* Pilot projects should precede national decisions, especially in programs of health, education, welfare, housing, etc.

N Revive the cabinet secretariat and use it for preparing inter-departmental options.

F* Replace the many clientele-oriented departments and agencies with a few, broadly based, goal-oriented departments.

F Have more press conferences at the departmental level.

? Encourage (or discourage) leaks if the leaker's conscience tells him to. Let the press then print it.

RELATIONS WITH CONGRESS

U* Restore the reorganization power to the President, by re-enacting the expired law.

F* A President will do well to recognize, work with, and take advantage of the strengths and constitutional checks of Congress, rather than attempt to by-pass them.

F The Government Operations Committees should "monitor the monitors" within Congress, by urging each other Committee (if it has not already done so) to set up a monitoring sub-committee for the Executive Branch units within its purview.

N Cabinet members should appear before one or both Houses of Congress for questioning. Perhaps these questions should be submitted in advance, and the sessions should be televised.

? Congress should establish a joint committee to oversee the intelligence agencies.

? Before inclusion of an item in his program, a President should normally take soundings in Congress. His party leadership and his congressional relations staff are vehicles for this.

U* The role of Congress in policy must be recognized and respected.

F Political appointees should maintain contacts with key Congressmen so as to nurture a continuous interchange of views — obviously only in so far as the Congressmen desire these.

F* The President and his associates should think of the localism in Members of Congress, not as a narrow parochialism, but taken in the totality of the membership, as providing a unique insight into the detailed texture of public opinion in the nation as a whole.

F* There is great difference of opinion as to how far, at what stage, and if at all, the President should bargain with Congress as to a given item on his program. It depends on the situation.

F* Policy decisions belong to both Congress and the President. In the end, the latter must yield, if he cannot marshal the necessary support or cannot work out a compromise or find a consensus, or have his veto sustained.

U   Use candor in dealings with Congress.

U* Congress must be strengthened.

F   Occasions will arise when a president will find it advantageous to challenge a hostile Congress by including proposals he knows Congress will oppose. He may then be able to capitalize on the opposition.

U   Members of the Executive Branch should be used in congressional relations during the period in which an element of the President's program is under active consideration in Congress.

THE BUREAUCRACY

U* The President must have a method or methods for handling interdepartmental problems, over-lap and duplication, jurisdictional disputes, conflict, failures in cooperation and effort.

U*Great and complex problems are normally inter-departmental. They will not yield to a series of isolated program efforts.

N Place a White House man in each agency, with the function of monitoring its responsiveness to the President's policy and directives.

U Staff attached to a unit's chief should be used for monitoring in carrying out decisions.

F Form a Federal Executive Service.

F* In general, a machinery should be available for promptly screening and settling minor matters in foreign policy without involving the President and others in the top echelon.

F* A "free lance" staff should be available, either on the 7th floor of State or attached to the NSC, or to the National Security Assistant, which should have the function of the fresh and free look at the material emanating from the regular hierarchical processes in State and Defense.

F An important new function probably is better initially as an independent agency. There may be exceptions.

F* Task forces and other independent evaluations can be used to develop alternative options to clientele-oriented existing governmental units and policies.

N Members of the career service should be banned from appearing before congressional committees.

N The Executive Branch should be constructed on pluralistic lines, so as to conform, by and large, to the congressional pattern.

? Retain duplication in the intelligence field, especially in estimates.

N Retain duplication in water resource management and construction.

U Do not invoke executive privilege to cover up errors in administrative decisions.

U Do not by-pass or violate Civil Service Commission regulations.

RELATIONS WITH STATES, LOCALITIES, AND REGIONS

F* Most social problems are in the field, and should be worked out in the first instance by Regional Councils.

U Locate departmental field offices as far as practicable in the same town.

F* Transfer more revenues and decisions to state and local units.

F* Consolidate under special revenue sharing most of the 1500 or so grants by category into a few broad functional grants.

?* Find ways and means for making less uniform and rigid federal regulations or incentives to states and localities. Allow more adaptation to local conditions.

F* Some interdepartmental committees belong at the field level, but these will need at least one neutral expert assigned to each.

? In lieu of general revenue sharing (all or part) transfer certain taxes to the states and localities, including the fixing of rates. Federal assistance in their collection may be used, if helpful.

RELATIONS WITH THE COURTS.

U 'A special prosecutor should be appointed to cover situations in which there is reason to believe that high officials may have broken the law and the Department of Justice is not trusted to prosecute. He need not be permanent.

N He should be permanent, or for a long term.

POLITICAL PARTIES

F A President should devote more attention to strengthening his party.

U* A good way to strengthen a party is to try to secure as strong candidates as possible for his party's congressional and gubernatorial nominees.

F We should try to build the two major parties into more meaningful protagonists in broad policy.

Index